A–Z OF NORWICH

PLACES - PEOPLE - HISTORY

Michael Chandler

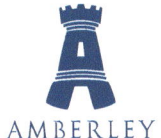

AMBERLEY

Dedicated to Ross

First published 2016

Amberley Publishing
The Hill, Stroud, Gloucestershire, GL5 4EP
www.amberley-books.com

Copyright © Michael Chandler, 2016

The right of Michael Chandler to be identified as the Author of this work has been asserted in accordance with the Copyrights, Designs and Patents Act 1988.

ISBN 978 1 4456 6224 4 (print)
ISBN 978 1 4456 6225 1 (ebook)

All rights reserved. No part of this book may be reprinted or reproduced or utilised in any form or by any electronic, mechanical or other means, now known or hereafter invented, including photocopying and recording, or in any information storage or retrieval system, without the permission in writing from the Publishers.

British Library Cataloguing in Publication Data.
A catalogue record for this book is available from the British Library.

Origination by Amberley Publishing.
Printed in Great Britain.

Appointed GPSR EU Representative: Easy Access System Europe Oü, 16879218
Address: Mustamäe tee 50, 10621, Tallinn, Estonia
Contact Details: gpsr.requests@easproject.com, +358 40 500 3575

A

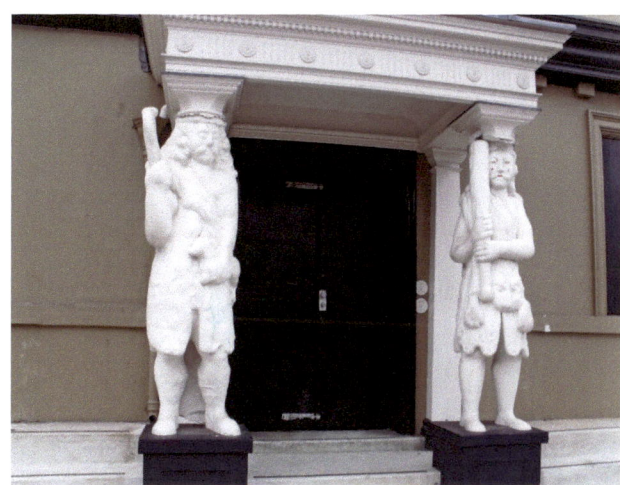

Samson the sturdy and Hercules the heavy.

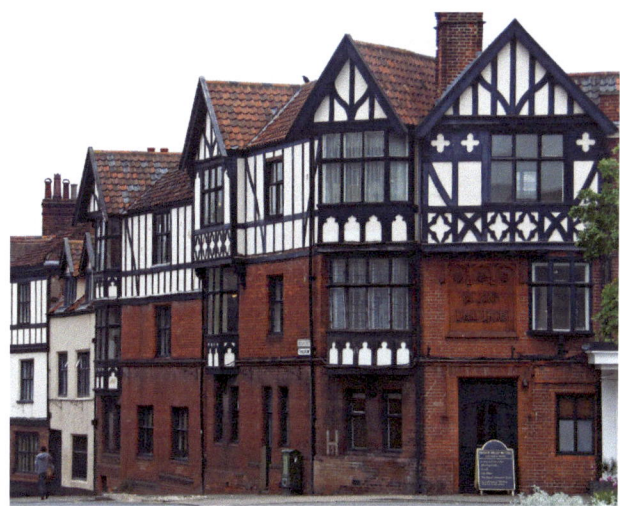

Maids Head Hotel.

'The Molde Fish Tavern' or 'Murtel Fish Tavern'. The names stayed until the reign of Elizabeth I. During the sixteenth century, the monks and citizens were always arguing about their rights and dues. In fact, in 1519, Cardinal Wolsey, under Henry VIII, came to Norwich to mediate.

In 1520, Catherine of Aragon was entertained at the inn, and during Kett's Rebellion, William Parr, Marquis of Northampton and brother of Katherine Parr, wife of Henry VIII, was ordered to quell the rebellion. He took breakfast at the inn before losing the Battle of Norwich to Kett's men.

The inn is mentioned in the famous *Paston Letters*.

The MAYDES HEDDE is recorded from 1472 when John Paston wrote to 'Mestress Margaret Paston, or to John Paston Esquire, or to Roose Dwyulling afoor there gate.' Regarding a visitor who would 'tarye at Norwich the whylys, it were best to settle hys horse at the Maydes Hedde, and I shall be content for their expenses'.

Coaches run from the Maids Head to London, and in 1762, Susan Nasmith and James Keith, joint proprietors of the Norwich Machine, state in their advertisement that their coach leaves the Maids Head for the Green Dragon, Bishopsgate, London at 11.30 a.m. on Monday, Wednesday and Friday. Four inside at 25s each and outside 12s 6d each with 20 lbs weight luggage.

Although the Tombland Fair was moved to Castle Meadow in 1818, it moved back in 1860 when the cattle market was having alterations. All sorts of attractions were there, including the Huttentot Venus, reported to be the strongest woman in the world. There you could purchase Diss bread, large flat square biscuits, Gibraltar rock and Tombland Fair buttons, which were round flat biscuits flavoured with either ginger or lemon.

Born in 1536, Thomas Anguish married Elizabeth Thurston and had nine sons and three daughters. Thomas took over his father-in-law Edmund's grocery business and became a freeman in 1573, now part of Maids Head Hotel, his house was situated here, and he became sheriff. When elected mayor in 1611, a pageant with fireworks took place when some fireworks went off unexpectedly and thirty-three people died trying to escape. A monument is above his seat where he worshipped in St George Tombland.

Thomas Anguish left the city a house for the teaching of poor children. It was set up in 1618 and then again in 1621 by a Royal Charter of Charles I who demanded that it be called the Children's Hospital in the City of Norwich of the Foundation of King Charles. The hospital closed in 1941 and is now Lakenham First School.

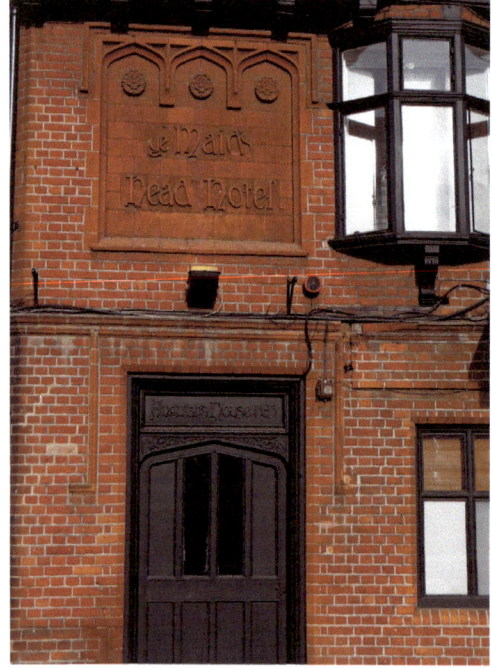

Thomas Anguish House by the Maids Head Hotel.

B

Bethel Street

Bethel Street takes its name from the Bethel Hospital that was founded in 1713. Most of the north side was demolished to make way for the Norwich City Hall.

In the early eighteenth century, Bethel Street was originally known as Over or Upper Newport Gate and then Committee Street, named after the Committee House, which was where the Bethel Hospital was situated. Committee House was blown up by accident with ninety-eight barrels of gunpowder during a tumult of 1649, killing and wounding one hundred people; this was caused by the refusal of the mayor to grant a petition presented by parliament for the entire removal of the images in churches.

The Bethel was one of the first charitable foundations in the country. On 27 June 1942, incendiary bombs destroyed Nos 53–57. Number 55 was at one stage the residence of Charles Burton Daveney, a solicitor of the Daveney family of Colton. Nearby, Watts Court that had an impressive carved archway, which was of Tudor origin, was named after the merchant John Langley Watts, mayor in 1774; he was also known as being the first mayor of Norwich to have two Christian names!

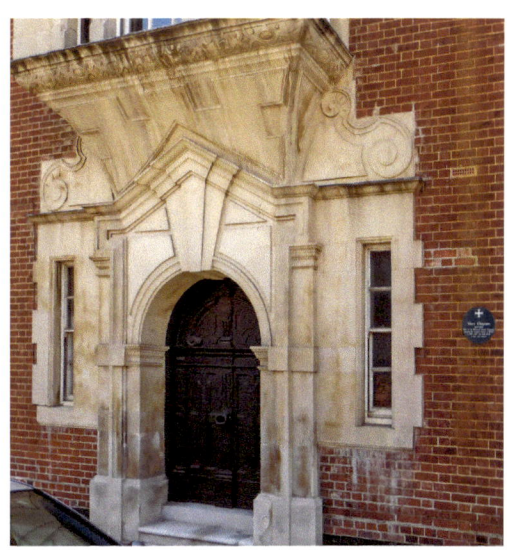

Bethel Street hospital apartments.

Mary Chapman was born on 24 March 1647 to Dorothy Fountaine and John Man who went on to become the sheriff and mayor of Norwich and also alderman and sheriff of London. Mary married Revd Samuel Chapman on 10 May 1682, and she went on to become the founder of a purpose-built mental hospital. Mary died on 8 January 1724, and the first meeting of the trustees took place four days later. It was requested by Mary that the word 'Bethel' was to be fixed over the front door with the text from Hebrews xii: 16: *but to do good and to communicate, forget not; for with such sacrifice God is well pleased.*

In Mary's will dated 1717, the pious clause stated,

> Whereas it has pleased almighty God to visit and afflict some of my nearest relations with lunacy, but he has blessed me with my use of reason and understanding; as a monument of my thankfulness for this invaluable mercy, I settle Bethel, &c for this purpose.

It also stated in Mary's will that she had no real estate to leave, but only a personal wealth to the extent of the sum of £3,513 1s 4d and the long lease of the Bethel that is now converted into a freehold. The Charity Commissioners' reports increased the amount to £13,101 13s 8d: an amount of £1,800, 3 per cent stock and £250 bank stock.

During the first meeting of the governing bodies, Sir Benjamin Wrench was added to the number of trustees by the following method:

> Whereas Mrs Mary Chapman of the City of Norwich, lately deceased, hath by her last will and treatment nominated and appointed seven persons to be trustees for the management of her charitable benefaction of the house of Bethel, whose names are inserted in her last Will and Testament and by a proviso in the said Will appointed that if any of the trustees therein named should depart this life before her demise and she does not in writing under her hand elect another person in the room of the deceased that then the by

The late Sir F. BATEMAN
Will.

Sir Benjamin Wrench was also appointed to be the physician to the Bethel on a yearly salary of £16. William Cockman, Esq., was appointed to be the treasurer on a yearly salary of £16. Finally, John Lombe at a yearly salary of £16 was appointed a clerk to the Bethel.

Robert Waller was appointed master to the Bethel to provide for and take care of the lunatics therein, and for that service 'he is for the present to be allowed for salary at the rate of £30 per annum'.

One of the earliest entries in the accounts is of the insubordination of Master Robert Waller who, upon being remonstrated with by the trustees, used several contemptuous expressions against the trustees declaring that he would not be directed by any man and that they might put another person into his place as soon as they pleased.

The trustees at this early period were not of a stamp to submit to such conduct, and it was therefore resolved that the said Robert Waller shall have 4s per week taken from his salary of £30 per annum, and this deduction to be continued during the pleasure of trustees.

On 27 May 1728, the first code of rules was adopted at this meeting as follows:

1) Any four or more Trustees and not fewer shall have full power to transact and determine any business or matter relating to this Hospital.

2) All business or matters so determined shall be deemed and taken to be as effectually determined as if the said business or matters have been determined by all the Trustees, provided every such determination be made by and with the consent of four of the said Trustees then present, appearing by their signing the same and not otherwise.

3) That upon every fourth Monday a meeting of the Trustees shall be held in this house, or else when by adjournment, and every such meeting shall be called a General Meeting.

4) If any of the Trustees shall at any other time have any business of moment to propose to the rest of the Trustees, a meeting shall be summoned, and every such meeting shall be called a Special Meeting.

5) That the keeper of this house shall give notice thereof to each of the Trustees two or three days before any such meeting is intended, whether General or Special.

6) Al resolutions agreed on at a meeting shall be entered by the clerk in a waste book before such meeting breaks up, and each of the Trustees the present shall set his name to such entry.

7) All resolutions entered in the waste book shall before the next meeting be again entered fairly by the Clerk in the Journal Book provided for that purpose, and shall be read over and examined before any other business is undertaken and then be again subscribed by each of the Trustees then present.

8) All workmen before they be employed on any accounts whatsoever, shall first be approved by the Trustees at a meeting.

9) The Treasurer shall not make any payment to any workman, or to any other person without the warrant first signed by the Trustees at a meeting.

10) No lunatic person shall be admitted by the Keeper without a warrant first signed by three or more of the trustees.

11) Every lunatic person shall first be examined by the physician belonging to this Hospital, and receive from him a certificate declaring such person fiit to be taken into this Hospital before such warrant is granted by the Trustees.

12) The Keeper shall direct all persons who come to see this House or any lunatic person in it to the box, and desire them to put in what money they shall think

fit to give for the relief of the poor lunatic person, but shall take no money of any person whatsoever for his own use.

13) The Keeper shall not let more persons come into this House at any one time than ten, nor permit any more to come in till the former are all gone.

14) The Keeper shall not let in any person either to see this House or to visit any lunatic upon a Sunday, except the Trustees, the physician, the apothecary, and such are sent by one or more of these, nor upon any other day but at the times following, that is to say between the hours of nine and eleven in the forenoon every day of the year, and between the hours of two and five in the afternoon, from the 25th day of March to the 29th day of September, and between the hours of one and four in the afternoon from the 29th of September to the 25th of March, Sundays always excepted.

Carpenter Richard Starling and Mason Edward Freeman built the hospital for the sum of £314 2s 6d. In 1813, James Bullard, who was employed as the master, was killed by patient Jonathan Morley with a scythe while gardening.

After the Second World War, the hospital became an annex to Hellesdon Hospital. It was an out patients' unit until 1974 where it continued as the Centre for Child and Adolescent Psychiatry; it closed in 1994.

The hospital today houses apartments with a plaque commemorating Mary and her achievements.

Number 53 Bethel Street was built during the last half of the Georgian Period. It was three storeys high with an attic. Many local notables had lived there, including Mr James Cuddon, a solicitor, who was also the founder of the Law Union Assurance Society, which was established in 1854.

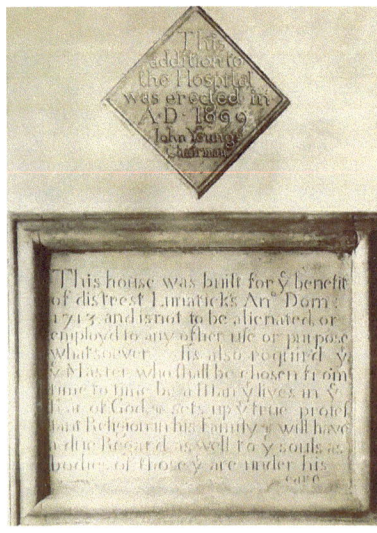

Bethel Hospital foundation stones.

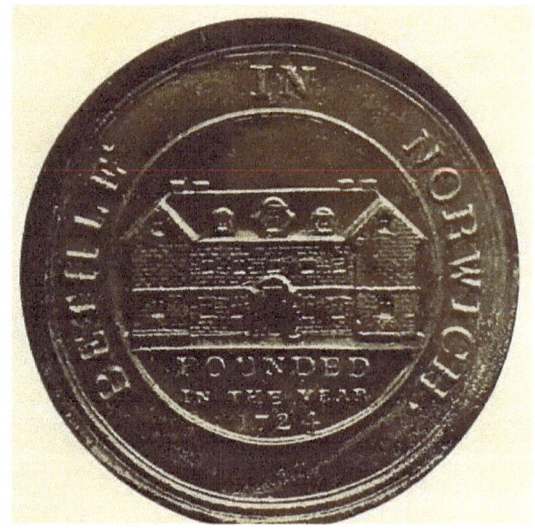

Bethel Hospital, seal of the hospital.

B

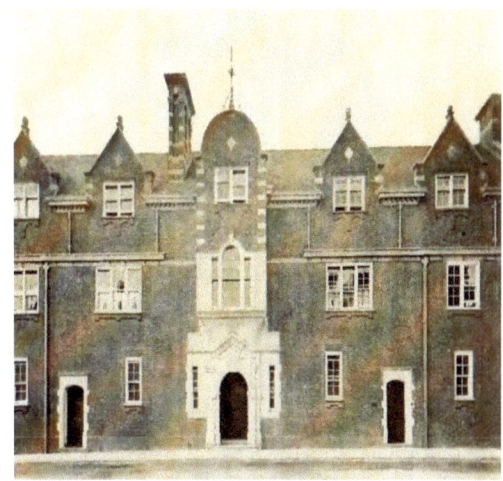

Bethel Hospital north front.

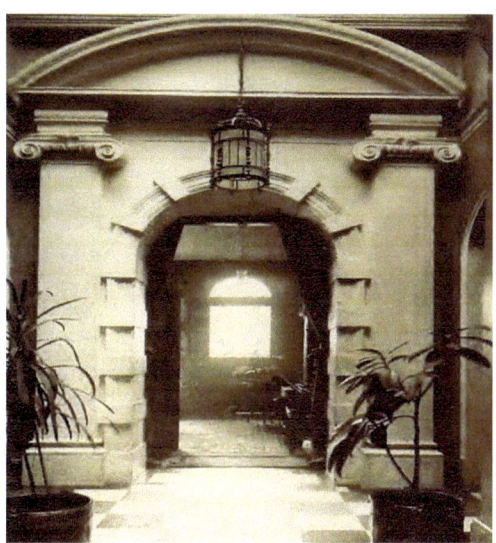

Bethel Hospital passageway.

James was the eldest son of Mr Tames Cuddon of Norwich who belonged to an old established Catholic family. On the death of Sir William Foster in 1874, James Cuddon was elected the Chairman of the Law Union Insurance Company, and when it was amalgamated with the Crown Life Insurance Company, he was unanimously elected Chairman by all his colleagues, both old and new. Called to the bar at Lincoln's Inn, he would always be remembered for his support of monasteries.

After this, Dr Edward Copeman, a physician at the Norfolk and Norwich Hospital, lived there from 1851 to 1878. He was also an accomplished musician playing at many Norwich musical festivals. Mr F. C. Bailey lived there in 1886, a surgeon and medical officer of the asylum for the blind in Magdalen Street. Just before the Second World War started, Dr G. S. B. Long lived there, and by 1940, the house was used by the Diocesan Refuge and then the house was destroyed.

A–Z of Norwich

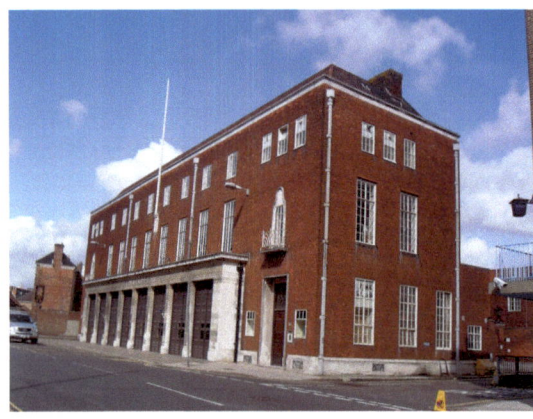

Bethel Street old fire brigade.

The old fire station in Bethel Street was designed by Stanley G. Livock of Norwich, and it was built by Simms and Cooke of Nottingham for £33,000. It was opened by the Lord Mayor Fred Jex on 9 November 1934. Work was somewhat delayed as the foundations of several wells were believed to have housed caches of arms and gunpowder from the Civil War.

Ninham Court, which took in 63 Bethel Street to 10c–11 Chapel Field North, was originally called Master's Court and renamed in honour of the artist Henry Ninham who was probably one of the lesser-known members of the Norwich School of Artists. He started as a copper-plate printer and became a skilful printmaker. His plates went on to be issued posthumously as fifteen items.

Richard Hearne was born in nearby Lady Lane, which today forms part of the Forum. His father Richard Senior was an acrobat, and his mother Lily May was an actress. Richard made his debut aged six weeks at the Norwich Theatre Royal, and he went on to become BBC television's first comedy star as the popular character Mr Pastry.

In 1926, he appeared at Alexandra Palace on the Baird System. Mr Pastry started from a stage show in which he starred with Fred Emney. It was called Big Boy. Mr Pastry went on to star in many children's and adult's slapstick sketches for stage, film and television.

In one sketch, he developed an idea from the comic Tom D. Newall, with his wife's permission. This is what Mr Pastry became famous for; it was called *The Lancers*, and the sketch showed Mr Pastry dancing ballroom style with an imaginary partner completely out of step. In 1954, he appeared in America on *The Ed Sullivan Show* and many bookings followed. The late great comic Billie Dainty did a great copy of this act.

Mr Pastry with the theme tune *Pop Goes the Weasel* lasted for twenty-five minutes, and Jon Pertwee from *Doctor Who* and *Worzel Gummidge* fame was one of the co-stars.

A film version was made that showed a darker side of Mr Pastry coming out of prison. Buster Keaton also appeared in the film with Mr Pastry.

Richard moved to the village of St Mary's in Kent in the late 1940s, and he always provided celebrities of the day to open up the local fete such as Ian Carmichael and Dulcie Grey.

B

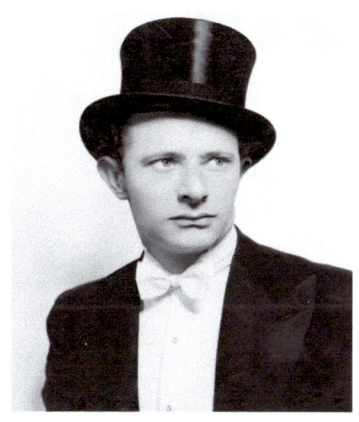

Young Richard Hearne – Mr Pastry.

In 1963, he became president of the Lord's Taverner's Charity. He was very active in raising money for therapy pools and was awarded the OBE for this in 1970.

Richard was offered the role of Doctor Who after the departure of Jon Pertwee, but he wanted to play the role as Mr Pastry, and the producer took away the offer instead giving it to Tom Baker.

But this was not the first time Hearne had dabbled with the idea of Doctor Who. For those of you of a certain age, you will remember the great comic actor Richard Wattis. The two Richards wrote a story about a man who could travel through time. The work was lost, and a few years later *Doctor Who* was born.

A young Petula Clark appeared in many of his films.

Richard Hearne died in Kent on 23 August 1979 aged seventy-one.

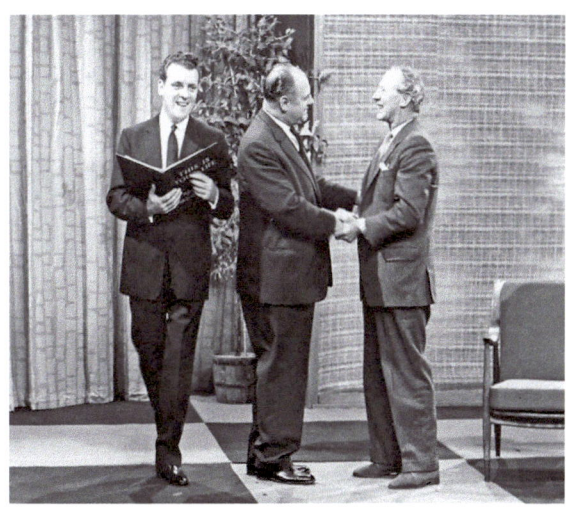

Richard Hearne was a subject on *This Is Your Life*.

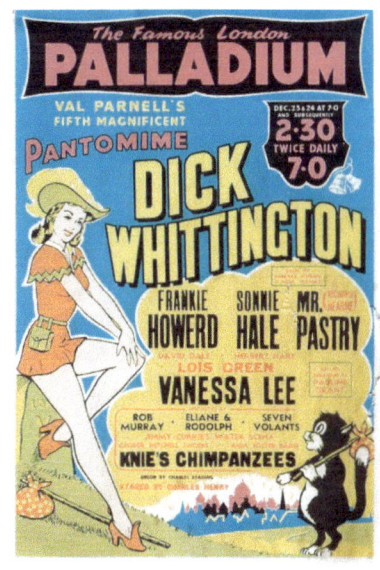

Mr Pastry poster for the London Palladium.

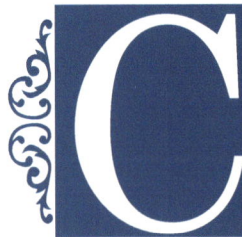

Caley's Chocolate

Albert Jarman Caley came to Norwich in 1857 and set up a chemist's in London Street, and within six years he was making mineral waters at the back of the chemist. The business expanded, and he moved into premises in Bedford Street. His son Edward J. Caley joined the company in 1878, and two years later, the Caleys took over a building in Chapelfield, which had previously been a glove cloth weaver.

In 1883, the company started to manufacture cocoa and started to produce chocolate by 1886. By 1890, a factory named Fleur de Lys was built on the Chapelfield site. Water was drawn from two wells being 400 and 500 feet deep. The company decided against importing chocolate from Switzerland and decided to make it themselves. They built identical plants and employed Mr G. Taylor to supply milk from his Whitlingham herd.

In 1918, the company was purchased by the African and Eastern Trading Company, and the Caley's division of mineral water and cider factories grew in London, Ipswich and Banham. The company then became unprofitable, and the new owners disposed of the business in the 1920s. During the same period, Lever Brothers purchased the Niger Company, and in 1929, the United Africa Company was formed by a merger of the Niger Company and the African and Eastern Trading Company and then Unilever was formed when Lever Brothers merged with Dutch Margarine Unie.

Richard Rout and Frederick Richard Rout started to produce cider and formed R. Rout and Son. In 1908, the company was sold to A. J. Caley and Son. Kelly Directory states that in 1916 cider was manufactured in Banham. By 1922, Frederick Richard Rout was shown to be living at the Cideries and was working from Hill Farm, Rosary Farm, Brickyard Farm, Eastlands Farm and Grays Farm. By 1933, Frederick had designed and built in Banham what was called 'The Garden of Eden Pleasure Gardens', which was a former disused earth pit covering 7 acres.

By the 1950s, the company was still producing cider and storing it in 10,000 gallon oak vats and 2,000 maturing barrels. By the end of the decade, Rout's cider works closed.

The artist Alfred Munnings designed most of Caley's advertisements, and their mineral waters were drunk by the Royal Family and Members of Parliament.

Albert died in 1895 after retiring in 1894, when Frederick W. Caley joined the firm along with Edward J. Caley and Stuart A. Caley.

C

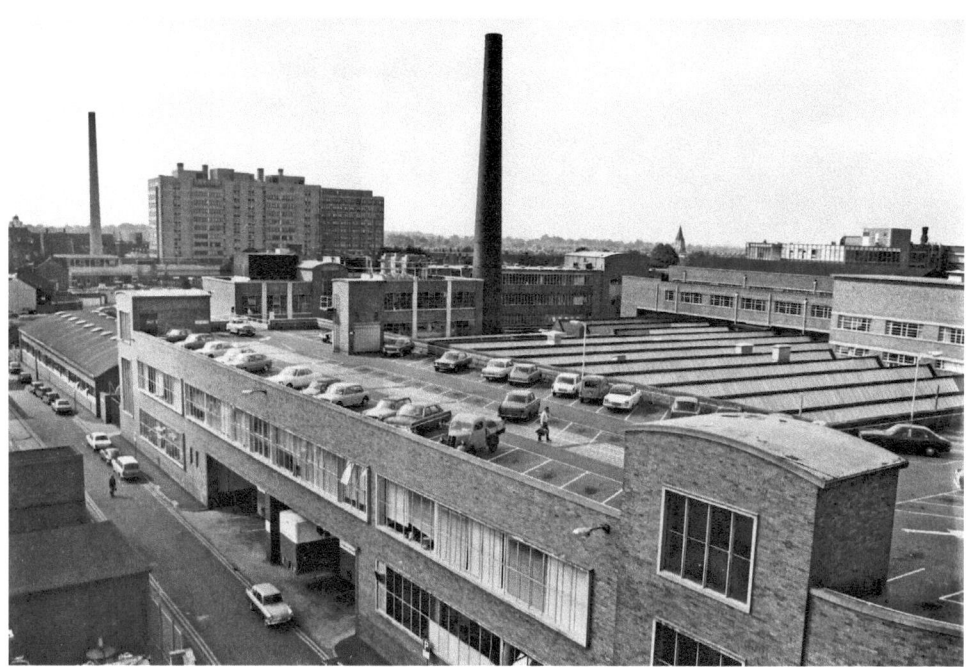

Chaplefield Caley's Factory.

Edward entered the City Council in 1895 for two terms, and in 1897, he was placed on HM Commission of the Peace for the city.

Caley's produced chocolate for the troops during the First World War, and it was named Marching Chocolate. Royal Warrants were granted for many of their products.

In 1932, Caley's was bought by John Mackintosh & Sons of Halifax, and in 1969, Mackintosh merged with Rowntree's and then Nestlé purchased the business in 1988, closing the Norwich site in 1994.

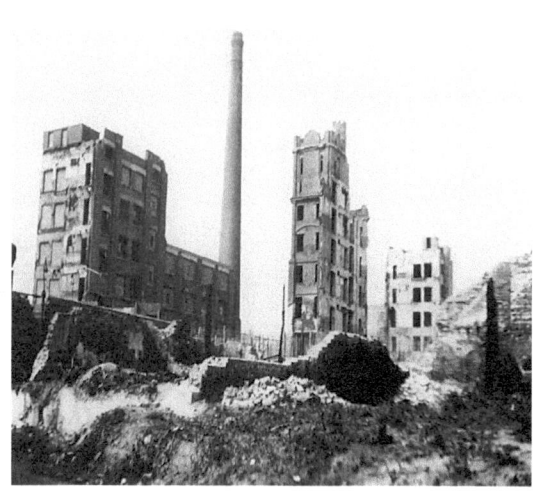

Caley's after the Blitz.

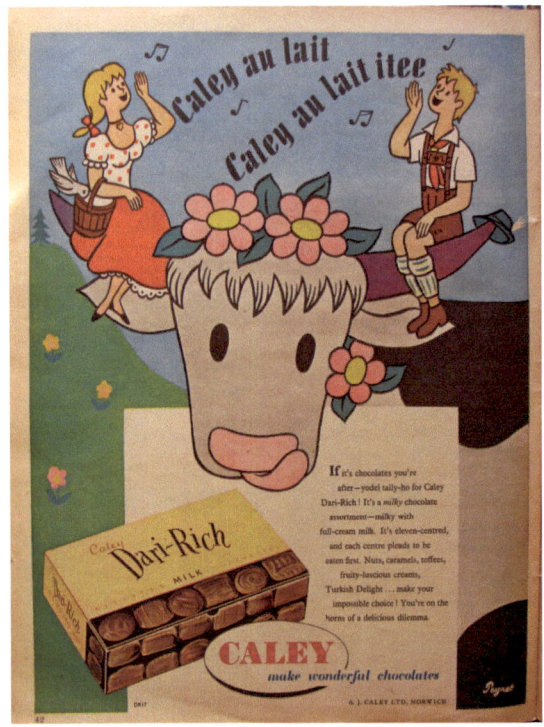

Caley's French flyer.

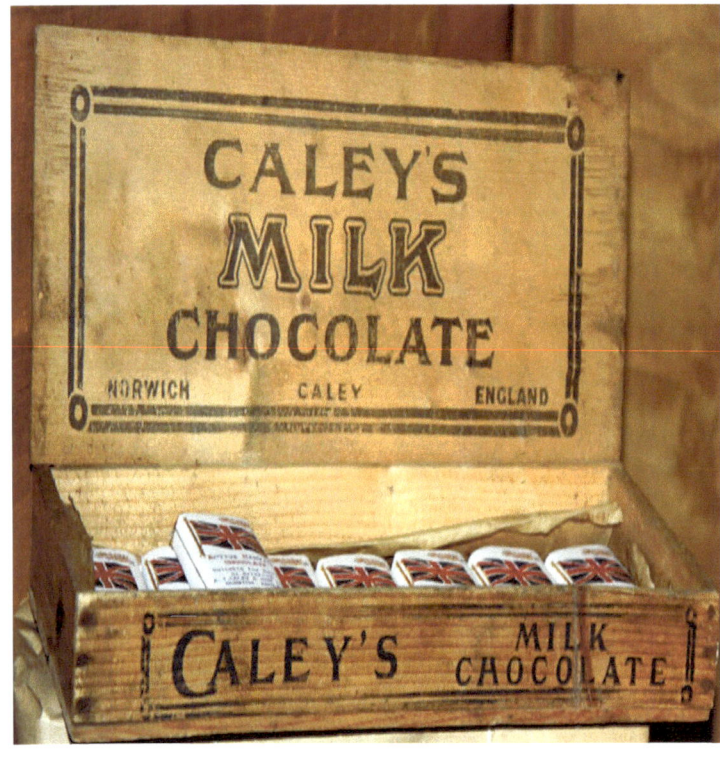

A crate of Caley's chocolate.

D

Duke Street

A public meeting was held on 18 October 1819 by adjournment at the Guildhall to take into consideration erecting a bridge over the river, near the duke's palace, to connect Pitt Street with the marketplace. A proposition to that effect was not passed, but a Bill for erecting the bridge was introduced into parliament and passed. Nearly £9,000 was raised by shares of £25 to complete.

Dukes Palace Bridge was opened as a toll bridge in 1822 and remained until 1855 when it was purchased by the City Corporation. It was built privately as part of a road scheme to link Charing Cross to Colegate.

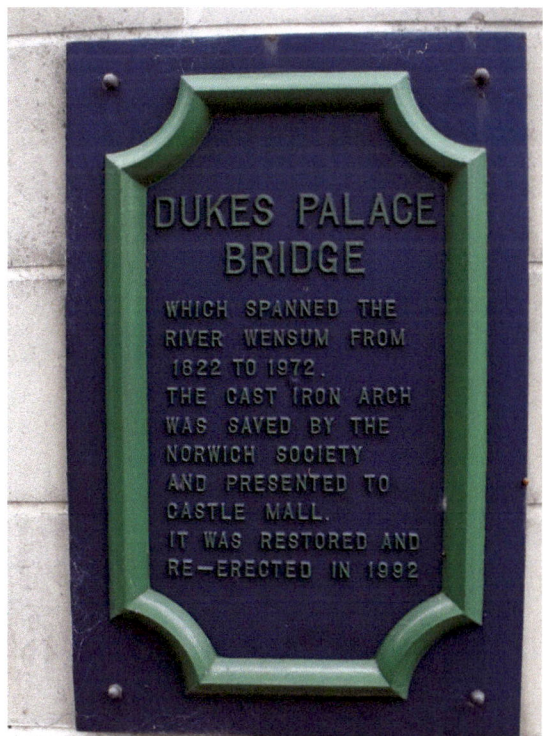

Dukes Palace Bridge plaque.

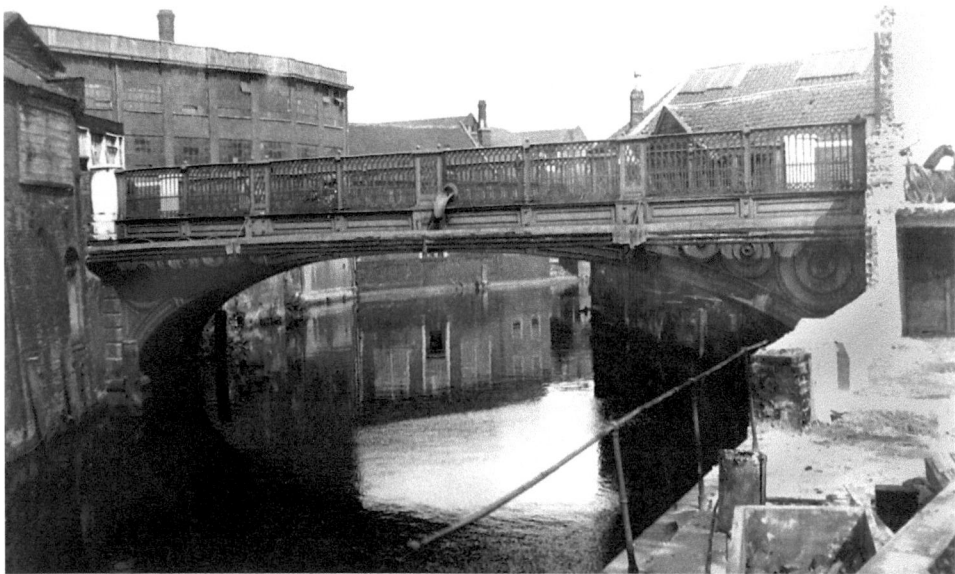

Dukes Palace Bridge.

An Elizabethan mayor's feast took place when the Earls of Northumberland and Huntingdon along with other noble persons went to visit the Duke of Norfolk and were entertained by him in 1561. The mayor was William Mingay.

At first, there was a great deal of opposition from local residents, but an Act of Parliament was passed, and the first stone for the Dukes Palace Bridge was laid on 28 August 1821. It was designed by Henry Lock and cast by John Brown. With a 60-feet elliptical arch and a pierced balustrade, and importantly, it became the last bridge to cover the Wensum within the city wall. Up until 1855, a halfpenny toll was imposed for those crossing by foot. It was then bought by the city for £4,000. The bridge was demolished when Duke Street was widened in 1972, and the cast iron arches were put up for sale and purchased by the Norwich Society; they were placed over the car park entrance on Rose Lane during the 1992 Castle Mall developments.

By the 1930s, the bridge was showing signs of wear and tear and had imposed on it a weight limit of 12 tons, and by 1972, this was reduced to 3 tons, and halfway through the year Duke Street was temporarily closed, and a new bridge was put in place.

It was stated that the Duke of Norfolk said, 'When I am in the tennis court of my palace in Norwich, I think myself as great as the King.'

The Dukes House stood from 1561 to 1711, and it was the largest house in England. At a Christmas Party of 1664, the evening was described by Thomas Browne as there being dancing through the night. In 1671, Charles II used the palace to entertain. In 1708, the Duke wanted his company of comedians to enter the city with banners, but Mayor Thomas Havers refused this so the Duke pulled down the palace and left the city.

After being used as a workhouse, it later became an electricity works, a brewery and is now a car park.

D

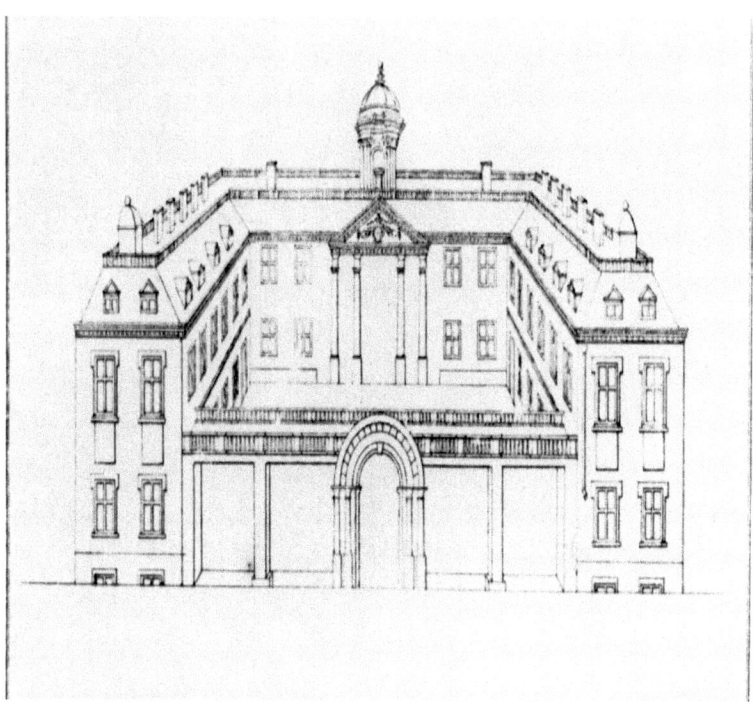

Duke of Norfolk's Palace 1720.

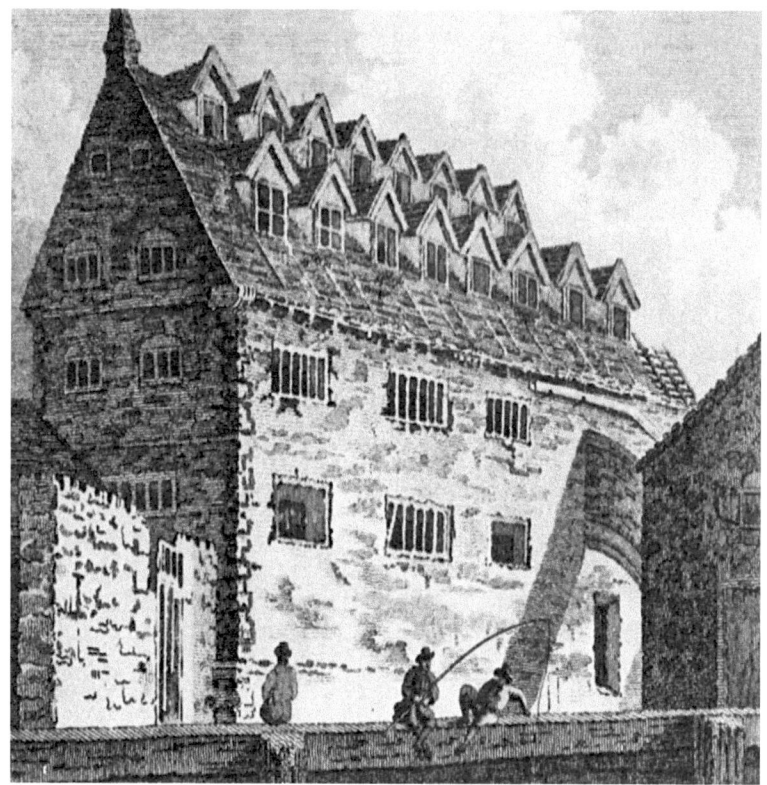

Duke of Norfolk's Palace.

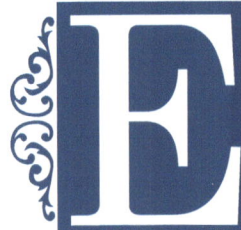

Eastern Counties Newspapers

In 1845, Jacob Henry Tillett had the idea of publishing a journal, and he shared his ideas with Jeremiah Colman, John Copeman and Thomas Jarrold. The *Norfolk News* was published in January 1845. It was first printed by Mr Josiah Fletcher and consisted of four pages and stayed that way until 1858 when it was printed by Messrs. Jarrold and Sons expanded it to eight pages at a cost of 2½d. The Colman and Copeman families still have a close involvement within the business.

The *Eastern Express* started in 1867, and by 1870, it was renamed the *Eastern Weekly Press*. Mr James Spelling was the editor from 1872 to 1897, and he also wrote about rustic life and provided the art work. In 1870, a four-page sheet came out under the name *Eastern Daily Press* with Archibald Cozens-Hardy as its editor, and during 1886, it became eight pages. The *Eastern Evening News* was released in 1882, and the company had two moves in 1902. They left the offices of Museum Court and the publishing offices in Exchange Street and the board of directors purchased a site in London Street, before moving to Prospect House in the late 1960s.

Eastern Counties Network was launched in 1996 to allow the company to move into Internet publishing.

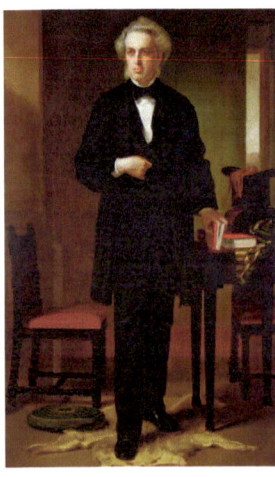

Jacob Henry Tillett, one of the founders of Eastern Counties Newspapers.

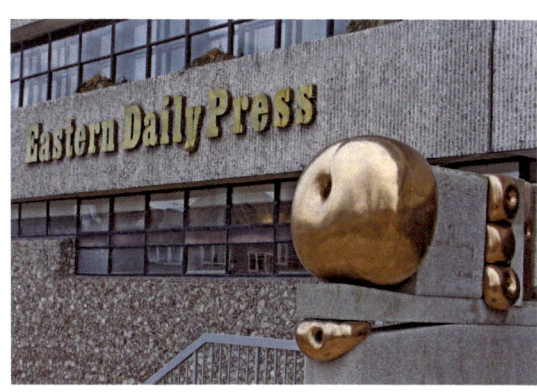

EDP Prospect House.

The company then merged with the East Anglian Daily Times Company to create Eastern Counties Newspapers Group (ECNG), and by April 1998, the group purchased Home Counties Newspapers Holdings PLC for £58 million, and it came with a range of twenty-six weekly paid and free titles covering the areas of Greater London and the Home Counties. In 1999, the company purchased Market Link Publishing for £5 million that included the monthly publication of *Professional Photographer*.

In March 2002, ECNG changed its name to Archant, and in December 2003, it purchased twenty-seven weekly newspapers from Independent News and Media in two deals that were worth up to £62 million. During 2005, magazine publisher Romsey Publishing Group was added to be part of Archant Specialists and also Highbury Local Publications that went on to form Archant Life and Archant London.

A merger took place in 2005 when Archant Anglia joined with Archant Norfolk and Archant Herts & Cambs, which is a division of Archant Regional. Archant Life Stable in 2006 added Metropolis Publishing's six titles of London Lifestyles, and it took over six country magazines from Advent Media in the Midlands.

In 2007, Archant sold its eight Scottish newspapers to Johnston Press for £11 million. By May 2010, Archant launched *Cambridge First*, a weekly newspaper, and it also acquired KOS Media Publishing Ltd in June 2010, KOS standing for 'Kent on Sunday'. By November 2011, the company became Archant Community Media Limited, but the group remains as Archant Ltd.

In 2012, iwitness24 community news platform was launched to transform the way news is collected by allowing readers to contribute. Continually going from strength to strength, the company acquired PlanningFinder, which is an online portal to search for planning applications.

By 2014, the company launched Mustard TV, broadcasting to Norwich and parts of Norfolk on Freeview Channel 8 and on Virgin Media. Archant now covers locations from East Anglia to Cornwall and Sussex to Yorkshire with many interests covered in newspapers and magazines.

Always keeping up to date, in July 2016, after the UK voted to leave the European Union, Archant announced a new pop up paper called *The New European*, which will have four editions.

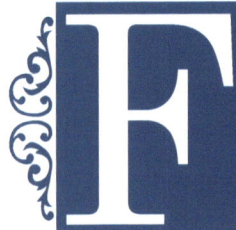

Floods

During its existence, Norwich has seen along with the floods, thunderstorms, hailstorms, whirlwinds and tornadoes. Thousands of people were forcibly washed away from their homes and even the cathedral was in danger of being destroyed.

In 1912, 7.5 inches of rain fell within a forty-eight-hour period making the city paralysed. It went up to 11.27 inches, which amounted to roughly half a year's rain. Many thousands of people were forced from their homes, and Norwich was totally cut off from all sorts of communications. Railways and the telephone systems were also in severe danger.

Houses were not the only buildings affected as the printing works of the Norwich Mercury situated in St George's had the two lower storeys torn out. The Boston Blacking Company on the other side of the river was left to fall into the river. Also destroyed were bridges at Trowse and Lakenham.

The damage was vast, with over 15,000 people abandoning their homes and nearly 4,000 buildings lost or damaged.

By the end of 26 August 1912, Norwich was virtually isolated from the country.

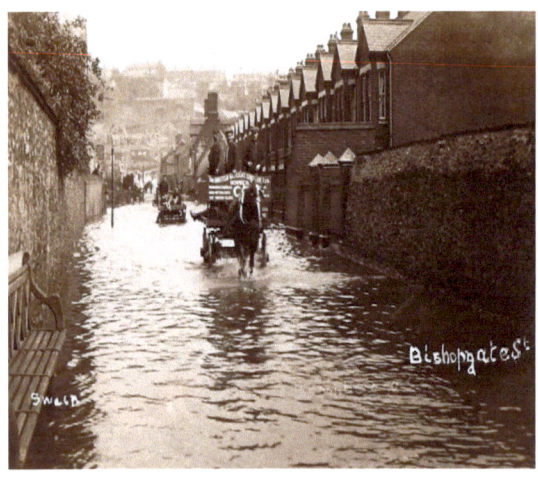

Bishopsgate Street flood, 1912.

Many people lost their lives. Ex-MP Mr Tillett and a serving police officer carried two nurses on their shoulders for 50 yards to a house to help a baby being born.

A relief operation then took place for many thousands of men, women and children who had become homeless, and seven schools were opened to assist. For those who could remain in their homes, blankets and food were delivered.

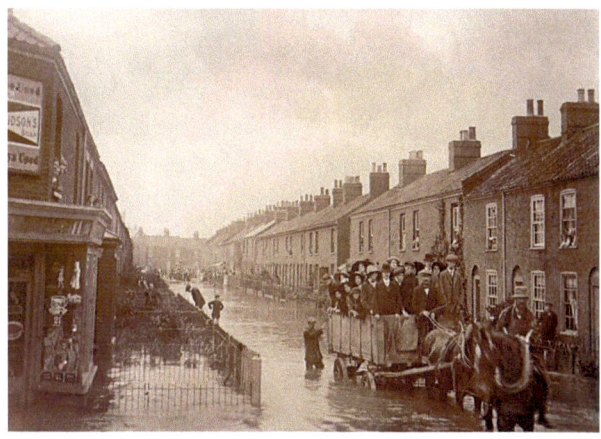

Devonshire Street flood, 1912.

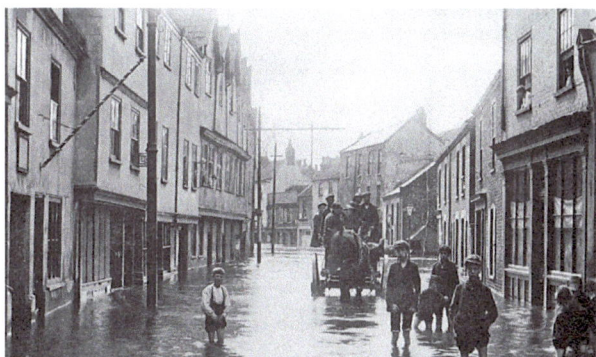

Oak Street flood, 1912.

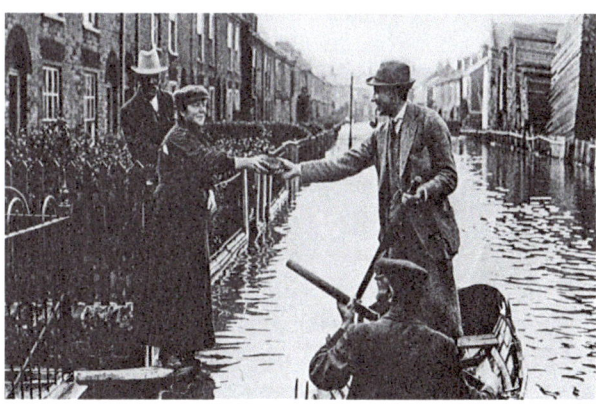

Westwick Street flood, 1912.

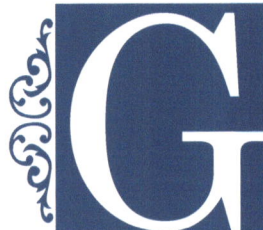

Gates

R. Fitch, Esq. was one of Norwich's leading authorities on the old walls and gates, and in 1861, he published *Views on the gates of Norwich*. In 1319, the walls of the city were completed, but neither the towers nor gates could be of use, unless furnished with items of war, and it was not until 1342, in the reign of Edward III, that a patriotic citizen named Richard Spynk gave 30 espringolds to cast stones to be kept at the gates and towers; he also gave 100 gogions (balls) of stone, a box with ropes and accoutrements, four crossbows and arrows, other equipment and armour.

Not only was the city indebeted to Richard Spynk for its safety, but also for the enhancement of its status. It was recorded that the king's mother, Isabella, induced her son, in consideration of the costs and charges for the walls, which had been raised without call on the government, to grant a charter to the citizens.

From the river to Coslany Gate, there were 112 battlements and 10 on the gate itself. From that point to St Augustine's Gate were 69 battlements and on the gate 12. Next to Fibrigge Gate – on the walls and towers were 153 battlements and on the gate 13; to Pockthorpe Gate – on the walls and towers were 178 and on the gate 10; and from here to the river were about 40. From here to the Tower of Conisford Gate, the river chiefly protects the city, but the tower bore 12 battlements; and from the tower on the city side of the water to Conisford Gate were 26 battlements with 14 on the gate. On to Ber Street Gate were 150; on the gate and its wicket were 27; and from here to St Stephen's Gate were 307; and on this gate and wicket were 28. From St Stephen's to St Giles Gate were 229, and on the gate and wicket were 15; from St Giles' to St Benedict's Gate were 100, and on the gate itself and wicket were 16; and on to Heigham Gate 79, and on the gate 4 – and from this gate to the Tower and Wall on the river were 16 battlements; in all 1,630.

According to the so-called Norwich Domesday, in 1345, there was a tax called *Fossage* to defray the great charge of the walls and ditches. By 1385, a survey took place and all the walls and gates were placed in good repair. Also at this time, churchwardens were chosen annually, and their duty was to prevent any decay or destruction of the fortification.

In 1386, the prospect of invasion was a real threat and the king sent 4,000 men to Yarmouth and Norwich and were told to place the walls, towers and gates in fit condition to repel those against the king's authority. This meant that the towers were filled with engines of defence, and the ditches made wide and as deep as demanded.

Richard Spynk and his male heirs were all given exemption from paying taxes to the city. He gave £200 5s, which in today's terms would be not far short of £30,000. A further number of funds were required to finish the work, and Richard offered a further £100 if it was matched. It wasn't, but he still offered the amount. Richard died on 30 July 1384, and parts of the ruins of the gates and walls are still seen today.

The accounts at the treasury for 1385 show that two labourers who were working at Westwyk Gates received the sum of 7s 6d and that also the sum of 5s was paid for a cart for a period of five days at Westwyk Gates and the sum of 15s 9½d was the fee for digging the ditch at Westwyk Gates. The sum of 8d was also paid for beer and for the carriage of a gun.

Between 1451 and 1481, West Wymer Ward took full responsibility for the repairs to the wall from the point of the tower on the north side of St Giles Gate following the walls and the towers to Westwick or St Bennet's Gate.

During Kett's Rebellion, the Earl of Warwick came into Norwich via St Benedict's Gate. Blomefield the historian stated that,

> unfortunately, carriages belonging to the army, loaded with ammunition, passed through these gates and continued across the city and straight out through Bishop Gate, delivering themselves, and their much needed ammunition, into the surprised hands of the enemy.

When Elizabeth I visited Norwich, the gates of St Benedict were decorated with cords that were made of herbs and flowers, with garlands, coronets, pictures and the richest of cloth.

In 1615 a Catholic priest named Thomas Tunstall was hanged, drawn and quartered. This took place on the gallows on Magdalen Gate, and his head was placed on a pole on St Benedict's Gate and his quarters were placed on other gates. Tunstall is a Catholic martyr and was beatified in 1929. Near St Benedict's Gate there were two inscriptions. One on the outside gate read:

TEMPORE HENRI WATTS
MAIORIS CIVITATIS NORWICH
ANNO DOM'NI 1646

The second one inside the gate on the tower read:

REPARATA TEMPORE
HENRICI CROWE ARMI
HUJUS CIVITATIS MAIORIS
1679

King Street Gate was repaired after an earthquake that took place on Christmas Day 1480, and the gate survived after Kett's Rebellion until 1664 when a part of it collapsed. It was restored and then demolished in 1794.

Ber Street Gate was weakened as well after the Christmas earthquake of 1480 and also burned during Kett's Rebellion. A further earthquake of 1580 caused damage. By 1720, it still had a bridge, and although it was plainly built, it was then rebuilt in a classical way before the gate was taken down in 1808.

Brazen looked like a miniature fort, and at the time of Kett's Rebellion, they reinforced the gate with beams that were destroyed by the Earl of Warwick. The gate was widened in 1726 to allow a coach and horse to enter. It was demolished in 1792.

St Stephens was the centre of attention when Elizabeth I was visiting Norwich in August 1578 as so much repairs were needed on the gates, which proved costly, but this was not the case when, on Thursday 28 September 1671, Charles II and his Portuguese wife Catherine visited. In 1793, the gate was destroyed and removed.

St Giles saw in 1789 more houses being built, and in 1792, the gate was removed.

St Benedict's was used by Henry VI to enter the city in 1448 and 1449, and Elizabeth Woodville, Edward IV's wife, came here in July 1469. The Earl of Warwick and his troops entered here during Kett's Rebellion. Demolition took place in 1793, leaving only the south side. It was destroyed during the Second World War.

Heigham Gate was in dispute between the Abbots of St Benet's Abbey with locals calling it 'Hell Gate'. It was demolished between 1792 and 1800.

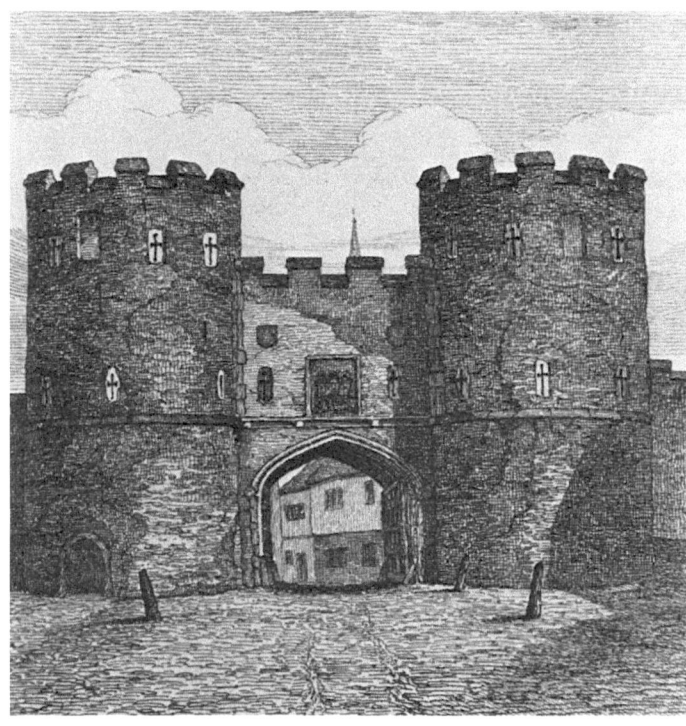

St Stephens Gate.

Coslany Gate dates back to 1275. In August 1549, the Earl of Warwick used this gate for him and his men to get out of the city and struggled to do so. Edward III used the gate with his wife Queen Philippa in 1340 to watch their son train for a tournament. In 1808, it became the last gate to be removed.

St Augustine's Gate was built in the early 1200s and demolished in 1794.

Magdalen Gate was built by 1339 and was the place of execution for thirty of Kett's men after the rebellion. The gate was removed in 1808.

Barre Gate was completed in 1339 and demolished in 1791.

Bishop's Gate was used by dignitaries to the Bishop's Palace and the Benedictine priory. The gate was attacked by Kett's men and it was rebuilt, but not as strong, and it was taken down in 1792. The bridge was saved from demolition in 1923.

The Water Gate had a house built on it. By the late 1500s, a succession of ferrymen were employed there, and it was known as Sandling's Ferry. By 1780, the canal was filled in and levelled. From 1790 to 1841, John Pull was the ferryman.

The Boom Towers were built in 1344 and given the name because a boom at some time did the same duty as the chain. In 1938, they resembled a devil with horns, and the turrets had fallen; it was known as the Devil's Tower.

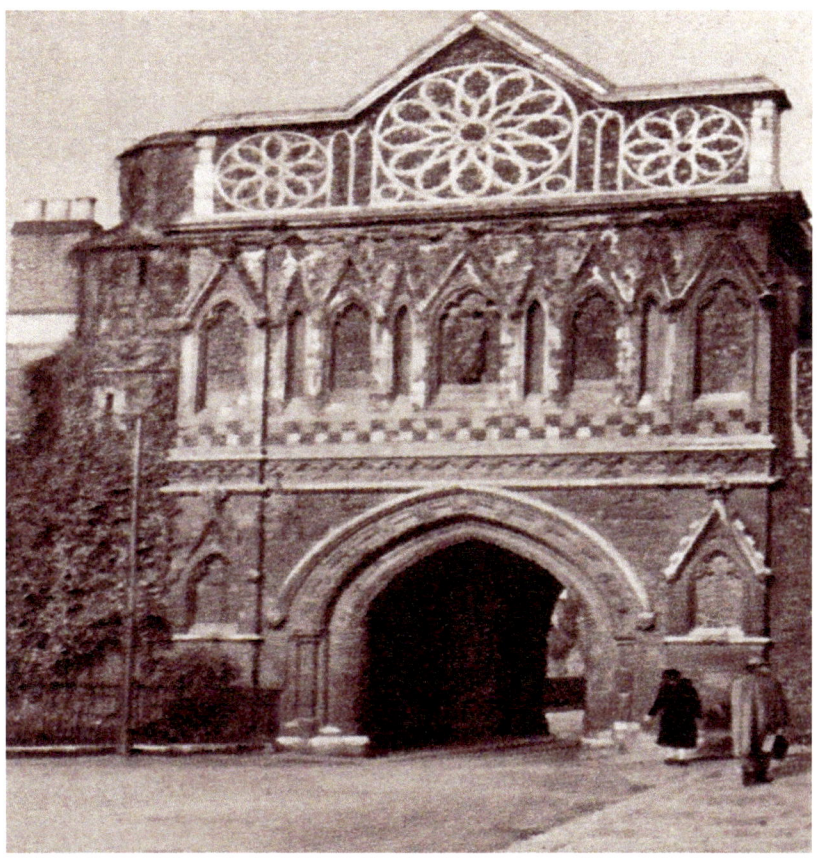

St Ethelbert Gate.

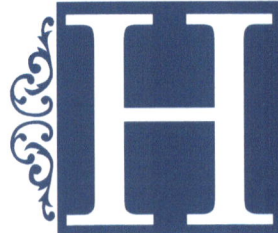

Haymarket

Meir Ben Aus Norwich was a Jew who lived in Norwich just before the edict that was laid down by Edward I. Meir wrote a series of poems that were lost for over 600 years and were rediscovered in the late 1800s in the Vatican Library. The poems were published in a book in 2013 called *'Into the Light': The Medieval Hebrew Poetry of Meir of Norwich.*

The Jews came to Norwich with William the Conqueror from France and the Rhineland under the king's protection. Along with York and London, Norwich became a city that had a Jewish population during the medieval period.

By the year 1144, a boy named William was found dead and the Jews of Norwich was blamed, and this became known as the 'Blood Libel' where Jews were accused of using the blood of Christian children to be used in *Matzo,* a form of un-leavened bread used during the Passover period.

There is very little known about Meir, and it is also not known if his writings were completed after the expulsion. It is known that one of his poems, where the lines are an acrostic, spells out, 'I am Meir, son of Rabbi Eliahu, from the city of Norwich which is in the land of isles called Angleterre. May I grow up in the Torah of my creator and in fear of him; Amen, Amen, Selah.'

At 3–4 Haymarket stands Curat House, which in its time was a spacious courtyard that led to an L-shaped house that also had an octagonal tower and a spiral staircase. The lower section of the property is flint, and the living quarters were lived in by John Curat and his family, while other parts of the house were occupied by his apprentices and servants.

During medieval times, this was the Jewish quarter. The synagogue and surrounding houses were burnt down in 1286. Named after Mayor John Curat, the Tudor house became known as 'Old Jewry'. The house was later owned by the Black family right up until 1971. It was a wine merchant's around the 1880s. It later became a tea merchant's showroom, and by the 1960s, it had spent time as a bar and restaurant. It was known as the Elizabethan rooms, but the original beams had been destroyed by a fire in 1962, the cellars were being rebuilt and a 50-foot well was capped. At a later period, builders found old glass, pottery and a box of bones, which turned out to be the bones

H

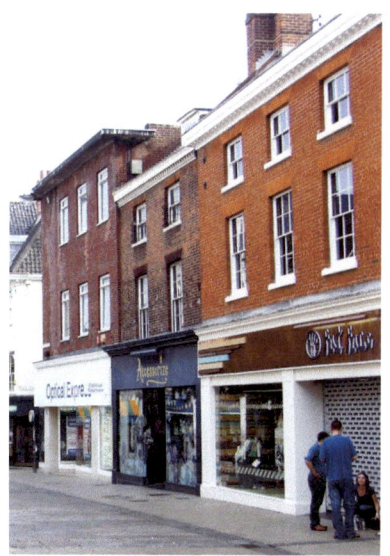

Curat House and the Medieval synagogue.

of Mrs Isaacs, and since then the building is said to be haunted by the Rabbi. Also destroyed during the fire was a doorway that had been replaced by the 1900s.

In one of the upstairs rooms, the logo of John Curat was found in the panelling, which consisted of a Q and a rat that formed 'Cu-rat'.

The Wind in the Willows feature was on the corner just by the shop where the statue of Sir Thomas Browne stands. It was placed in 1905 to mark the tercentenary of his birth, and is now placed alongside a sculpture of a brain, eye, seats and benches, which were commissioned by Norwich City Council from the artists Anne and Patrick Poirier.

Browne was born in London on 19 October 1605 and went to Winchester and Pembroke College in Oxford, and it was while he was in Ireland that he decided to study Medicine at Montpellier and Padua. He wrote the book *Religio Medico*, and then in 1637, he settled in Norwich, living in a house where Pret A Manger is now situated. The property was pulled down in 1842, and there is a plaque stating that Sir Thomas Browne lived here. He would later go on to write among others *Pseudodoxia Epidemica, Hydriotaphia, Urne Burial* and *The Quincuncal*.

A doctor and a naturalist, Browne was the owner of a stuffed dolphin and was a friend of the diarist John Evelyn, who went on in great detail to discuss his house and garden in his diary.

Thomas was one of the first people to write about the Norfolk dialect, and in his tract, *Of Languages and Particularly of the Saxon Tongue*, he wrote about and identified the words 'Mawther' (woman or girl) and 'Stingy' (mean).

Sir Thomas was buried in the nearby St Peter Mancroft after his death on 19 October 1682, his seventy-seventh birthday. By accident in the year 1840, his coffin was opened and his skull was removed, and it was then presented to the Norfolk and Norwich Hospital where it remained until 1922. Browne wrote many memorable nuggets and what is of great interest is his quote, 'To be gnawed out of our graves, to have our skulls

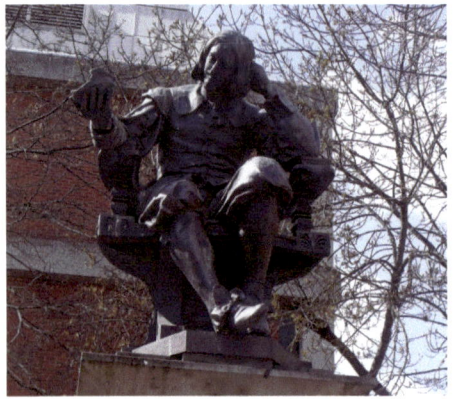
Sir Thomas Browne statue.

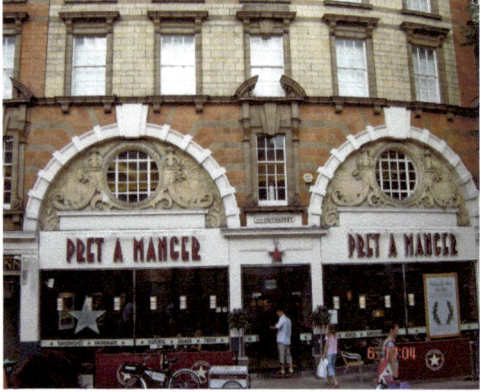
What was once the home of Sir Thomas Browne.

made drinking bowls and our bones turned into pipes is a tragical abomination.' How true this was for Browne.

John Aggus, innkeeper of 21 Haymarket and landlord of the Lamb Inn, was known as the storytelling landlord, and he told stories to children about fairies and pixies. During a cold day in November 1787, John's sister and her husband Timothy Hardy (also mentioned as Thomas Harder) turned up at the inn and in the kitchen area a row took place. Timothy pulled out a knife and stabbed John in the stomach, ripping his belly by up to 4 inches. He them attempted to take his own life, but failed. Timothy was charged with murder, hanged and sent for dissection. The ghost of John is said to haunt the inn with the last sighting being in 1999. Over the years, a photograph of John has been kept hidden with staff refusing to touch it, but now it is proudly fixed on one of the walls in the downstairs area.

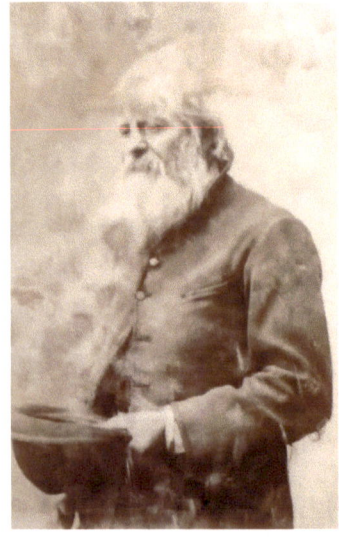
John Aggus, landlord.

I

Independent Jurisdiction

The Cathedral – Priory Precinct

Priory Precinct was the site that the first Bishop of Norwich, Henry de Losigna, acquired. This was an unusually large site, as well as seeing the site as a cathedral, but also for a priory for up to sixty Benedictine monks and an episcopal palace. Part of the eastern section was a meadow, but it is stated that some of the western parts were built on two churches that had been demolished. According to a complaint regarding the 1253 ditch, the meadowland, which was known as Cowholm, and also land on which the St Michael church stood, did not become part of the hundreds of Norwich. The Prior's Fee included not only the close, which is east of Tombland and south of Holmestrete, but the whole of Tombland and the settled area along Holmestrete, Normannesland and Great Newgate. The people who lived in these areas lived their lives under jurisdiction separate from the rest of the city.

The Great Hospital

The Hospital of St Giles was founded by Bishop Suffield in 1249. The hospital took care of ill priests who had no premises to reside in. There were thirty beds for the sick and other parts of the hospital were used to feed the poor on a daily basis. It soon went on to become a home for the wealthy citizens who wished to retire there.

The Castle Fee

When construction first took place, over ninety-eight burgesses lost their homes. The fortification was the single royal castle in Norfolk and Suffolk, and the mound at the time was the highest of any English castle. The fortification became much stronger in the late twelfth and early thirteenth centuries when the city took over the fee, and the keep and the mound were extended.

The Shirehouse

This is where the county court was held by the sheriff, and as a result, this remained outside the city jurisdiction even though it acquired the surrounding fee in 1345.

Normannesland
This area of land was part of the Prior's Fee and was also known as Spitelond. Arguments were caused by the 1253 ditch, as the area was never part of the hundreds of Norwich. It had a hospital that was dedicated to St Paul, but also known as Normanspitel. By the first part of the twelfth century, new endowments covered the areas northwards and new settlers, including a parish church, were found and the hospital became known for looking after poor invalids.

Great Newgate
This was agriculture land that was once called Thedwardscroft. The name 'Newgate' came from the name of the street on which it lay, which was an offshoot from Nedham Street. It was also part of the Prior's Fee. After arguments on ownership between the city and the priory, the king took it from the priory in 1291 and handed it back to the city in 1305.

Little Newgate
These were fields that were held by the Carrow Abbey. The Abbey held Leet Court for all the tenants, but went to hand over its jurisdiction to the city in 1290. The name came from being nearer to the lower and lesser part of the street that was known as Newgate.

Pockthorpe
This was a manor that was part of the Prior's Fee and was extended to cover the northern bank of the river. It was also a home for the Cathedral Priory. The 1253 ditch was purchased by the Carmelites for their friary.

Carrow
The Abbey was founded in 1146 by a grant of the king to a group of Benedictine nuns, but this set the scene for many future jurisdiction disputes. One dispute was the nunnery's claim for their right to collect a toll on all the corn that was sold in the city during the Carrow Fair.

Chapel in the Fields
The chapel held a large site by the middle of the thirteenth century. At one stage, there was a hospital present, but before the 1253 ditch was dug, it was transformed into the Collegiate Church of St Mary's that looked after a community of priests.

Jarrold

The Jarrolds came to England with William of Orange in 1688, and it was John Jarrold who, at the age of twenty-five, started the business in Woodbridge, Suffolk, in 1770. But after five years in business he died, and after his death, the business was placed in the control of trustees for a considerable amount of years, and in 1785, John Jarrold's son John became involved within the business.

A printing press was established and *Tracts for the Times* was printed. The next items to be printed were *Poole's Illustrated Bible*, *Cook's Voyages* and *Burkitt's New Testament*. From the middle to the end of the twentieth century, Jarrold Printing was one of the foremost colour printers in Europe, printing many high-quality and long-run books, magazines and mail order and industrial catalogues.

At its height, the company employed up to 1,600 staff. In the early years of the twenty-first century, there was overcapacity in the printing industry and technological advances made it very competitive.

Jarrold decided to sell its printing and publishing activities and concentrate on its retail property, business training and business services activities. The main property development site is the 17 acres at St James Place. The spirit of the company's printing heritage continues at the John Jarrold Printing Museum.

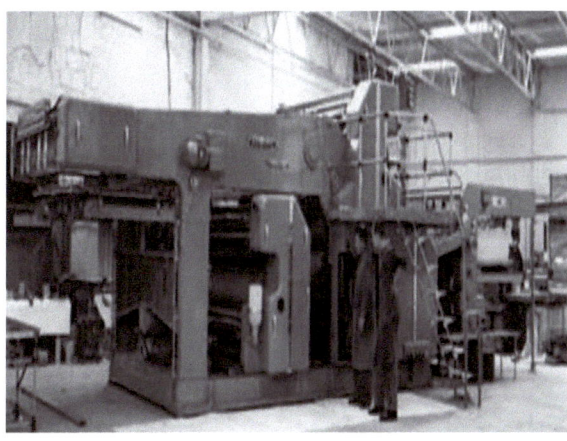

Ambassador sheet-fed single colour litho press.

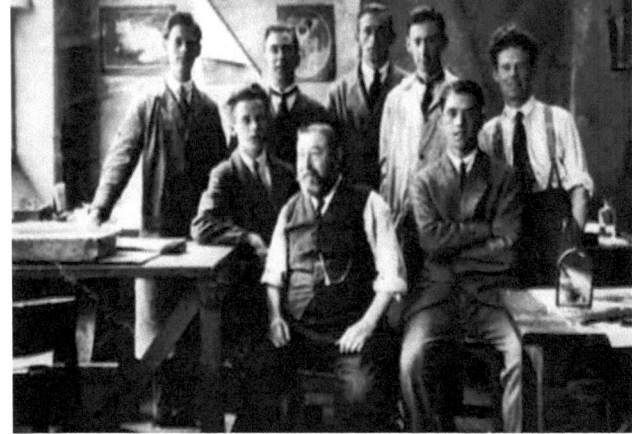
Jarrold lithographers 1922.

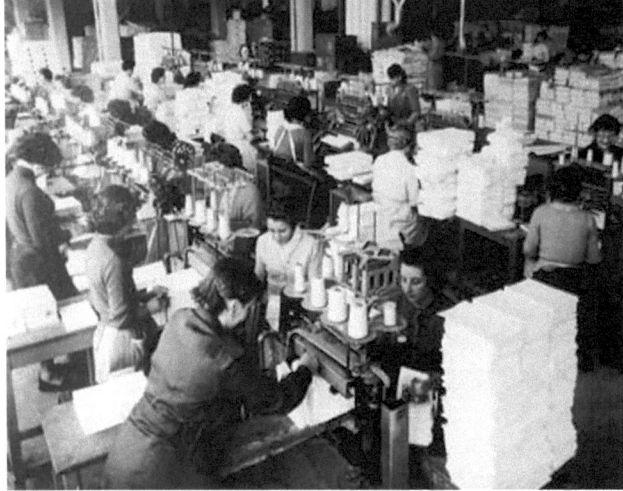
Jarrold bindery c. 1960.

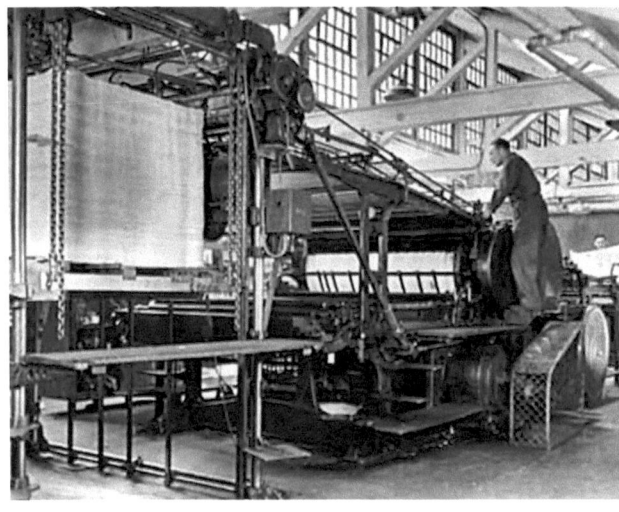
Letterpress machine from 1950.

In 1823, John along with his son John James moved to premises in London Street, which was then known as Cockey Lane. In 1825, the other son Samuel Jarrold became a partner in the business, and in 1831, his son William Pightling Jarrold joined, and a year later, another son Thomas Jarrold joined. John Jarrold Jr retired in 1848 and died in 1852.

The company continued printing text books, including the Tonic Sol-fa System that was originally put together by Sarah Glover in Norwich.

The Jarrold family devoted a lot of their time to public work. Thomas was a member of the Corporation of Norwich, Income Tax Commissioner, and he sat on the board of management of the Norfolk and Norwich Hospital. By the time the Education Act became law, Jarrold's saw the circulation of their education series grow.

In 1880, Samuel John James Jarrold took over the business from the trustees. The business soon had a Royal Warrant as school stationer to the Prince of Wales. Soon a new breed of directors took over, those being William Thomas Fisher Jarrold, Thomas Herbert Curtis Jarrold, William Hucks Webster and John Edgar Moorhouse. Other branches were soon established at Cromer and Sheringham.

Jarrolds.

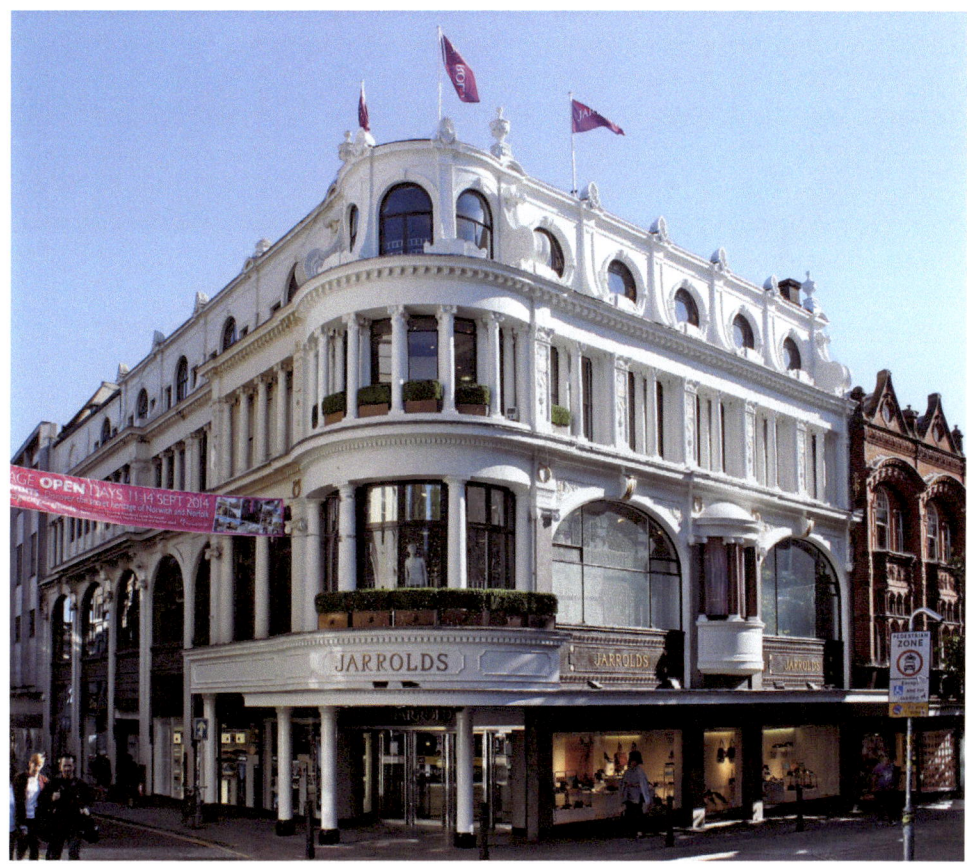

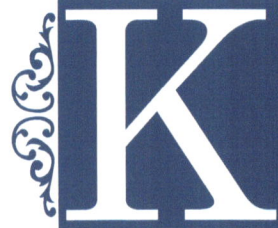

King Street

King Street goes from Bracondale to the Prince of Wales Road and is the oldest street in Norwich. Saxons settled here along the river bank near the old Roman Marching Route where King Street became part of a route to the north. During the 1980s and 1990s, it became rundown, but during its time it has had many merchants and has been an important thoroughfare.

By 1146, the city's only female religious house, the Benedictine Carrow Priory, was founded here and in the 1300s the Augustine Friars moved here.

Dragon Hall was built in 1427 by wealthy merchant Robert Toppes, in which he displayed goods he had imported from Europe. The hall is reputed to be the only remaining trading hall in Western Europe built by an individual.

Robert was mayor four times, but he was also banned from the city for a year for his part when in the 1430s merchants from Norwich tried to resist interference from outside the city.

He was married twice and had two sons and six daughters. His other business interests included being a mercer and textile merchant. Because of shipwrecks and piracy, Robert went into partnership with men called Pygot and Clyd to share the financial responsibilities.

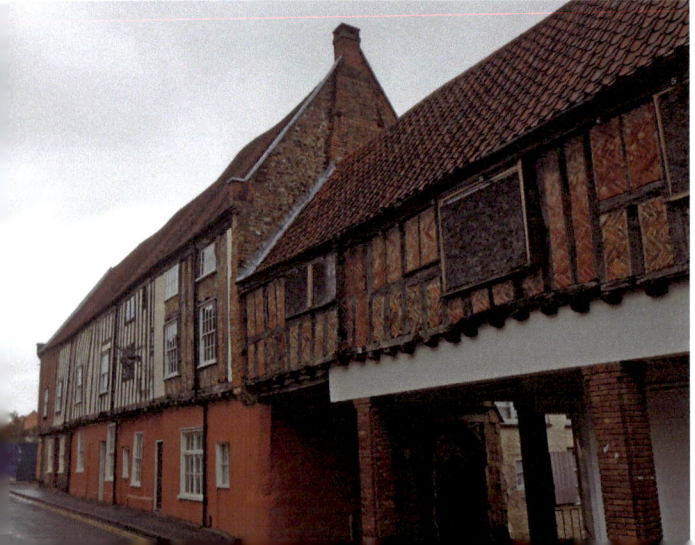

Dragon Hall.

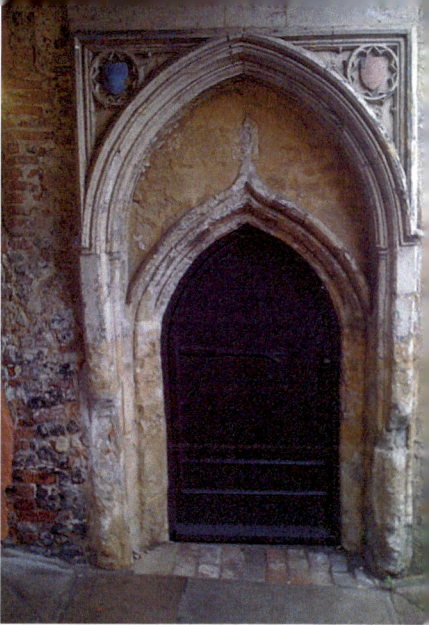
Dragon Hall doorway.

The original Great Hall was 15 metres long and the centrepiece measured 26 metres in length and had 14 dragon carvings made from Baltic oak.

When Robert died in 1467, the Great Hall ceased to be a trading centre, and for over a period of one hundred years, it came to be a residential house for the gentry. It was around this time the Guild of St George was formed, and on the feast of St George, a procession went from King Street to Tombland with Snap, a brightly coloured hobbyhorse with dragon wings and snappable jaws. This remains the city's symbol, and the regalia can be seen in the castle.

By 1619, trade and industry became very important in King Street and the gentry moved back to their country seats.

By the twentieth century, the Great Hall was turned into six properties, five dwelling sand a public house. From the 1960s, it was all change again as the street level became three properties with one tenant being Swatman's Butchers. A slum clearance took place in 1965, and it left only three cottages behind. The building was later owned by Watney Mann's Brewery who sold it in 1979 to Norwich City Council. The Norfolk and Norwich Heritage Trust was opened in the same year and work began returning the building to its medieval roots, and it was opened to the public in 1987. By 2004–05, the Hall was given £1.8 million for redeveloping and was opened in 2006 as a major attraction where among weddings, business meetings, concerts and functions also take place.

Jews' House (or Music House as it is known today), as historians have stated, was built by John Curry, who was also known as John, son of Herbert. It was later rebuilt by Jurnet, a Jewish merchant, money-lender and as some believed the richest man in the kingdom. During this time, the Jews were fined heavily by the kings of the day. Isaac, son of Jurnet, took over the house and became richer than his father. He died in 1235, and the property was divided among his children. His son Moses had three sons, Abraham, Hake and Jurnet. On the death of Moses, the property was divided among the three sons. By 1253, Hake was imprisoned in the Tower of London and converted

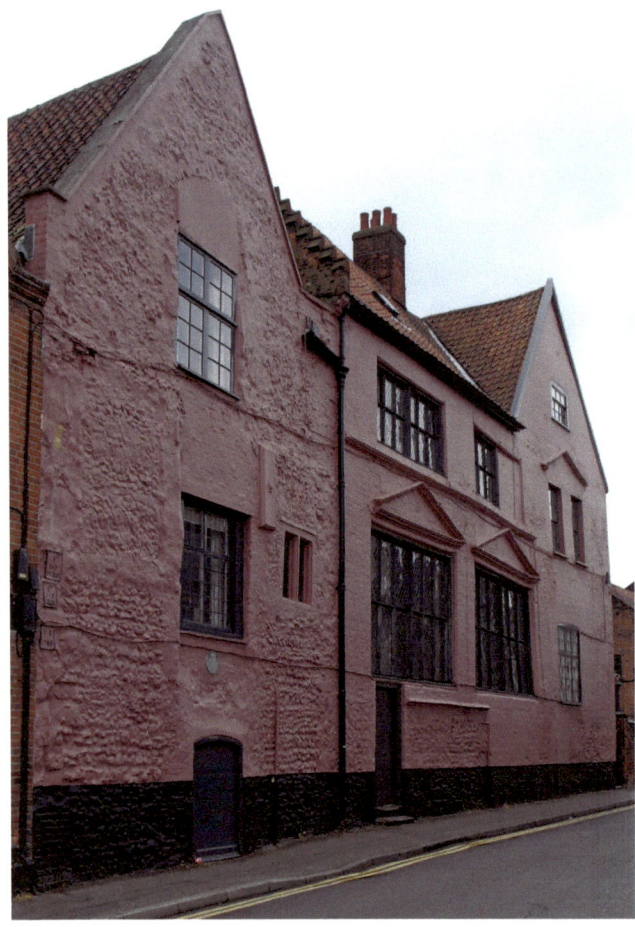
Music House.

to Christianity. Abraham died in 125; he had held property in London, Ipswich and a messuage in Saddlegate, which is now White Lion Street. The house today forms part of Wensum Lodge.

John Kaye, or John Caius, as he is commonly known, was born in Norwich in 1510, and he studied in Gonville Hall, Cambridge. He took his degree of MD in the University of Padua and was appointed principal physician under Edward VI, also looking after princesses Mary and Elizabeth. His name was later appended to the college that he studied at, that being Gonville and Caius Hall.

At the time of Kett's Rebellion, Mayor Thomas Codde was held hostage. He also lived nearby as did the parents of painter John Cromes, who were landlords of the Griffin Inn.

Hildebrond's hospital situated on the west side of the street was founded in 1216 by a mercer called Hilderbrond le Mercer and his wife Maud. It was later the building for the Norwich Brewery. The hospital came under the ancient parish of St Edward, and the bishop was given the title of patronage. Hilderbrond and Maud later built for the use of the

K

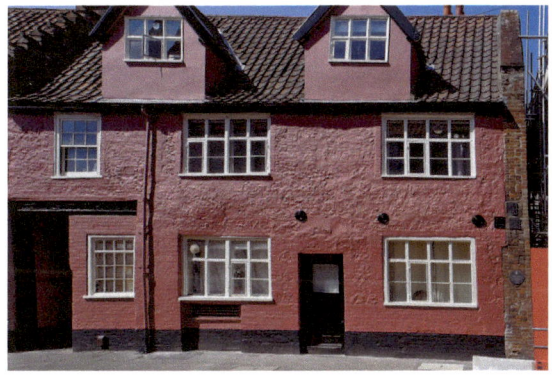
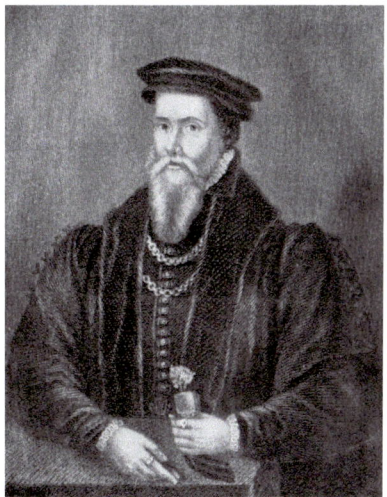

Above: Caius House.

Right: John Caius.

brethren and occupants a chapel that was dedicated to the honour of St Mary, and in time, the church became closer to the hospital, and the parish united it to the church of St Julian.

During the fourteenth century, a register of the archdeaconry of Norwich, known as the 'Norwich Domesday', contained the following entry, which was cited by the historian John Kirkpatrick:

> There is in the parish of St Edward a certain hospital called Hildebronde's Spytelle, lying near the churchyard on the south side, built with houses and a hall, and chambers for the master, in which said hospital, poor people wanting lodging ought to be entertained, and to have a certain quantity of fuel (focalium) from the master.' It is further stated that the master had a chapel to St Edward's church, where he would celebrate mass at his pleasure. The annual value of the hospital was estimated at 100s. The information of the cathedral paid the hospital a rent of 2s 6d; the city paid it 7s 6d for stalls in the market; and the hospital of St Giles 2s.

The masters of the hospital were as follows:

Nicholas (fn. 55) rector of Bernham, 1262
John de Royng (fn. 56) died 1290
Thomas de Mutforde (fn. 57) appointed 1290
John de Wykelwoode (fn. 58) appointed 1320
Robert de Langele (fn. 59) resigned 1353
Henry de Plumpstede (fn. 60) appointed 1353
Peter Mighel (fn. 61) presented by the king, 1385
John Eyr (fn. 62) presented by the king, 1385
John de Elmham (fn. 63) appointed 1397
Willliam Friseley (fn. 64) appointed 1401

John Haukins (fn. 65) appointed 1405
John Bowd (fn. 66) appointed 1412
William Hayton (fn. 67) appointed 1413
William Toby (fn. 68) appointed 1419
Roger Malmesbury (fn. 69) resigned 1471
Thomas Massen (fn. 70) appointed 1471
John Jollys (fn. 71) 1497
Thomas Deye (fn. 72) 1504
John Underwood (fn. 73)

Howard House takes its name from Henry Howard, the brother of the Duke of Norfolk, who went on to succeed his brother as the 6th Duke of Norfolk. The property went on to become listed in 1954 and then again in 1972, when it was made Grade II listed because of the undercroft, which English Heritage says is fifteenth century with two bays of brick, three chambers and two end chambers with evidence of internal and external stair entrances.

The garden was well known as 'My Lord's Garden', and it was built over during the nineteenth century. The house was near to Synagogue Street that has long been demolished. Synagogue Street was the only named street of its kind in England.

As restoration work at Howard House continues, a letter has recently been found dating back 130 years. The contractors discovered the letter under the floorboards and gave it to Norfolk Record Office for safe keeping and then it was opened. It was addressed to Miss Spencer who is thought to be a family member of Dr Christopher Spencer, a surgeon living at Howard House. The letter is believed to be a message of condolence signed by G. Dye and dated 8 February 1884. The seventeenth-century house belonged to Henry Howard, 6th Duke of Norfolk and had been empty for over twenty years.

Milling in Norwich became a tradition and the company at the top of its field was R. J. Read Ltd. The founder, Robert John Read, came from Wrentham, Suffolk, in 1851. Robert died on 3 October 1920, and the business became a limited company with directors being Robert John Read Jr, Lewis Hector Read and F. G. Turner.

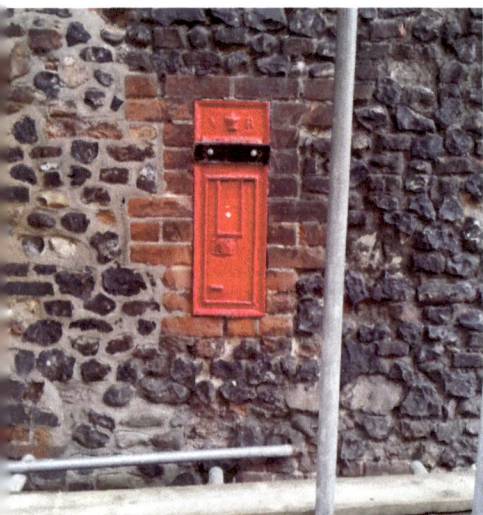

Howard House.

From the 1940s to the 1980s, the company moved in four different directions. The Norwich grain business expanded and the growth of the animal feed contributed to the expansion of industry, as did imported maize. The company was importing over 1,000 tons each week, but this ceased on the joining of the Common Market as home-grown cereals became cheaper.

In 1965, the Woodrow flour business merged with Reads and became R. J. Read (Holdings) Ltd and Read Woodrow Ltd. All production was then done at the City Flour Mills, the former Albion Mill.

Sadly, this great company closed in 1993 and stood derelict until 2004 when it was purchased by P. J. Livesey Ltd and converted into flats.

By the year 1200, King Street had eleven churches, and in a short period of time, many churches were added.

In 1842, the Wardens of St Julian's repaired the hassocks for 8s 6d, the roof in 1844 for £12 8s and then in April 1845 in the early hours of the morning nearby neighbours heard the crash of the eastern wall collapsing. So bad was the incident that at one stage it was believed the church would have to be demolished. The cost to repair was £600 with a six penny rate levied towards the cost.

Interesting lists of bell-ringing costs come from St Peter Southgate where it states the following:

November 9, 1810 For tolling the bell on the day of Princess Amelia's interment – 12s
1837: Bell for King William's death – 12s

St Peter Southgate also showed the costs for a rather expensive social occasion:

For beefsteak dinner at the Dreadnought on the day of the Perambulation – £1 5s 3d
Kett: beer – £1 2s 10d
Clabburn: cakes – £1 0s 0d
Linstead: beer – 10s 3d
Buttle: beer – 6s 8d
Use of a boat for going bounds – 1s 0d.

At one stage, St Peter Southgate and St Etheldreda's shared the Revd J. Bishop.

Some of the services in the churches of King Street were used to highlight the danger of Rome, and the sermons were published as *Anti-Catholic Pills*, aimed at preventing people from converting. Another sermon was against the Calvinists who were found in a chapel in Bishopsgate that was owned by the Countess of Huntingdon, and it was called 'An Exhortation to the Inhabitants of St Peter Parmentergate not to follow fanatical preachers'. The vicar, who was said to have also delivered part of this sermon to the cathedral at St Andrew's Hall in an attempt to convert the Jews, would have been well aware that nearby Synagogue Street housed a synagogue.

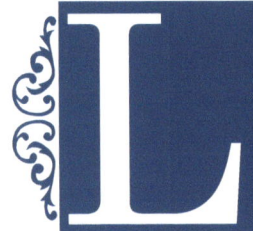

Lollards' Pit

Lollardy, known also as Lollardism, Lollardi or Loller, was a religious movement that survived from the mid-fourteenth century until the Reformation. It was first set up by John Wycliffe, a theologian who was expelled from Oxford University in 1381 for his criticisms of the church that were placed in his doctrine of the Eucharist. His ideas and that of the Lollards were to reform the ideas of Western Christianity.

A group of Lollards took to parliament with what was called 'The Twelve Conclusions of the Lollards' and attached them to the doors of Westminster Hall in 1395. The list contained the Lollard ideas.

The main points of Lollardy were that the Catholic Church was corrupted by temporal matters and that being the one true church could not be justified by its heredity. Lollards were also iconoclasts, believing that the funds spent on church artwork could go to the poor and needy.

The Lollards were classed as heretics, and it led to Wycliffe and the Lollards being protected by some of the nobility, including John of Gaunt, who had used the doctrines to their advantage to gain a source of revenue from the churches. Even though Wycliffe had been removed from Oxford University, it also protected him on the grounds of academic freedom.

The first time the Lollards faced persecution was just after the Peasants Revolt in 1381, and it was then that the nobility that housed them, when royalty found them to be a threat against the church and society. This was exacerbated by the fact that by 1386 John of Gaunt had left England to fight for the Crown of Castile.

Lollardy was fervently opposed by Thomas Arundel, Archbishop of Canterbury, and his hatred was echoed by Henry le Despenser, Bishop of Norwich.

In 1410, John Bradby refused to renounce Lollardy, and he became the first layman to be sentenced to capital punishment in England for the crime of heresy.

Many other martyrs were executed for refusing to renounce Lollard causes, including the Amersham Martyrs in the 1500s and that of Thomas Harding, who in 1532 was one of the last Lollards to be made a victim. Lollards' Pit is where men and women were burnt.

L

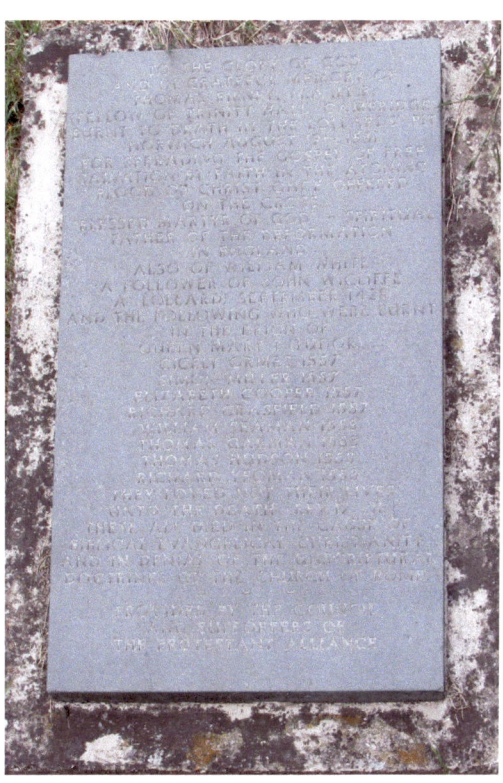

Lollard's pit.

Thomas Bilney was an English martyr whose preaching contributed to the reformation of the church in the sixteenth century. Thomas came to Norwich to preach in the open air, the reason being that he was without licence to do so in a church. He distributed Tyndale's English translation of the New Testament, which was banned by the authorities. Back in London in March 1531, he was arrested and taken back to Norwich and was convicted as a relapsed heretic. He was imprisoned in the Guildhall where there is now a plaque, and on 19 August he was taken to Lollards' Pit.

During his last night housed in the Guildhall, Thomas tested his powers of endurance by holding his finger in the lighted flame of a candle to prove his willingness to suffer his approaching doom.

Many sympathisers and friends were there. Bilney told the crowd that he was truly sorry for preaching without a licence, but stated that he denied teaching heresy. He was then burned at the stake.

What is interesting is that in 1534 Bishop Nix was condemned for executing Bilney without state permission.

In March 1556, one William Carman of Hingham was burnt to death, having been charged with being an obstinate heretic and actually having in his possession a bible, a testament and three psalters in the English tongue. In the same year on 13 July, Simon Miller from Lynn and Elizabeth Cooper, a pewterer's wife of the parish of

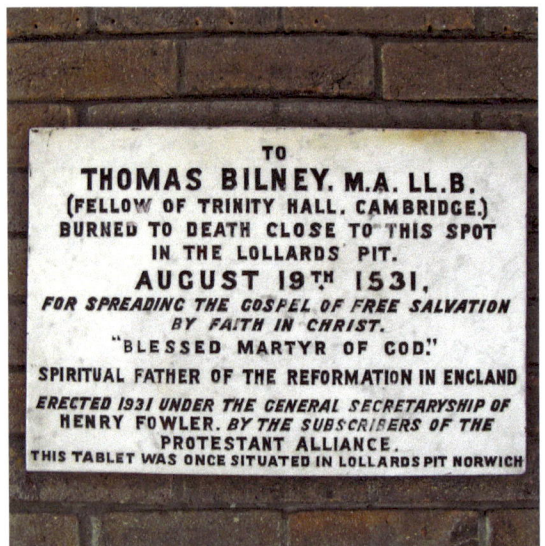
Thomas Bilney.

St Andrew, were burnt together to death, and on 5 August, Richard Crashfield, from Wymondham, Thomas Carman, William Seaman and Thomas Hudson were burnt for heresy. On 10 July 1557, seventy-year-old devout minister Richard Yolman was burnt for heresy.

Bishop Hopton and Chancellor Dunnings' instigations sent several martyrs to the reformed religion to be burnt between 1557 and 1558.

But what happened to the Lollards? During the English Reformation, they became part of Protestantism.

M

Magdalen Street

By the medieval times, Magdalen Street was home to migrants and refugees. The area was filled with courts, one being Twinemakers, which was a long alley that housed private courts.

By 1959, a makeover was produced for the area winning the first Civic Trust award for regeneration. The name 'Stump Cross' was a reference to a stone cross that stood at the spot during the fifteenth century. The cross was damaged many times, and it became known as the stump. It was moved to St Saviour's church where it survived to the nineteenth century.

Botolph Street started from St Augustine's Street to Magdalen Street, and it was all but removed in the 1970s for Anglia Square. Named after the medieval church that stood between Botolph Street and Magdalen Street until it was destroyed in 1549 – one of the finest buildings, some say in Europe. Robert's Printing Factory was also destroyed after being there since 1903.

Excavation in 1987 of the medieval cemetery of St Margaret's on Magdalen Street: revealed 436 skeletons and the remains of 600 more.

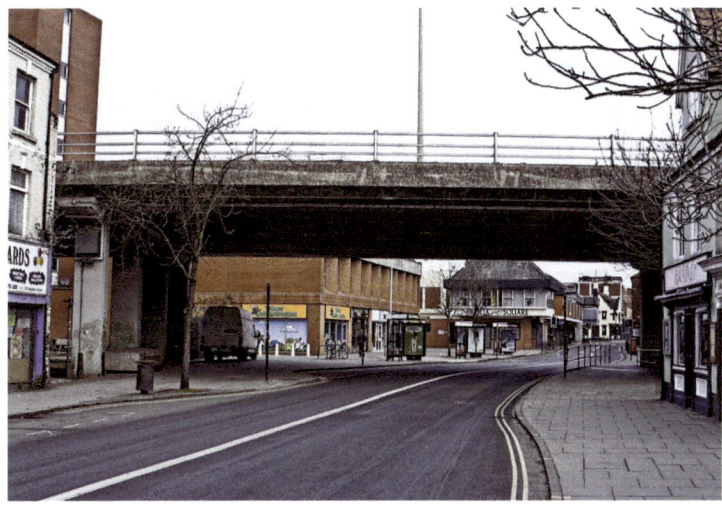

What was Stump Cross.

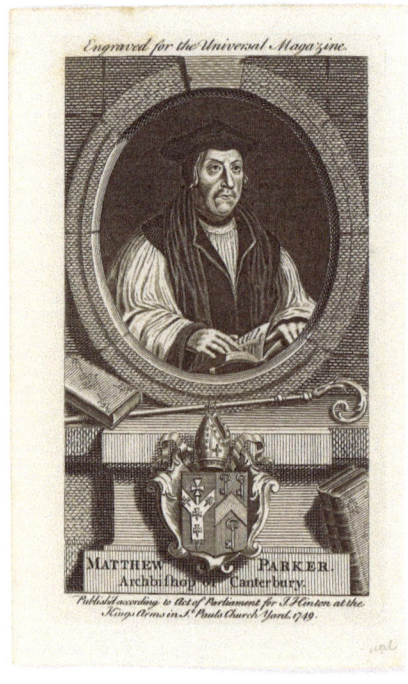

Matthew Parker, Norwich resident, Archbishop of Canterbury and allegedly the original nosey parker.

St Botolph, St Botulph or St Botwulf was a church that was named after a seventh-century abbot and saint. The original Botolph or Buttle Street is long gone. It was here that Stump Cross joined Magdalen Street. Present there was the Norwich Odeon that was a 1930s art nouveau picture house. Chamberlin's clothing factory was also situated nearby. Evidence shows that there was an early gate on Botolph Street.

St Botolph was a Saxon noble and East Anglian saint associated with travel. He built a monastery before he died at Iken, not far from Aldborough.

No. 19 Magdalen Street was once part of an old public house. When it was owned by the company Radio Rentals, staff said that the shop was haunted and that a figure had been seen at the foot of a flight of stairs, and that draughts had been felt. When a new company took over, the staff claimed that they heard footsteps and felt coldness, even where no windows had been left opened. One member of staff claimed to have seen a typewriter working on its own.

Archbishop Matthew Parker, born on 6 August 1504, was the son of a wealthy citizen called William. He was educated at the grammar school in Norwich and sent to Corpus Christi Colleague in 1520. He gained his degrees of BA, MA, and DD before 1538. Made Archbishop under Queen Elizabeth I, he instigated unpopular inquiries into the clergy and thus it was, it was thought, got the name nosey parker. The story is probably false. He died on 17 May 1575 and was buried in Lambeth Chapel. During the Civil War, his remains were dug up and left in a heap and reburied after the war.

The Norwich Crape Company Ltd 1856 was situated in Magdalen Street and Botolph Street. Founded by John Sultzer who became a director along with Edward

M

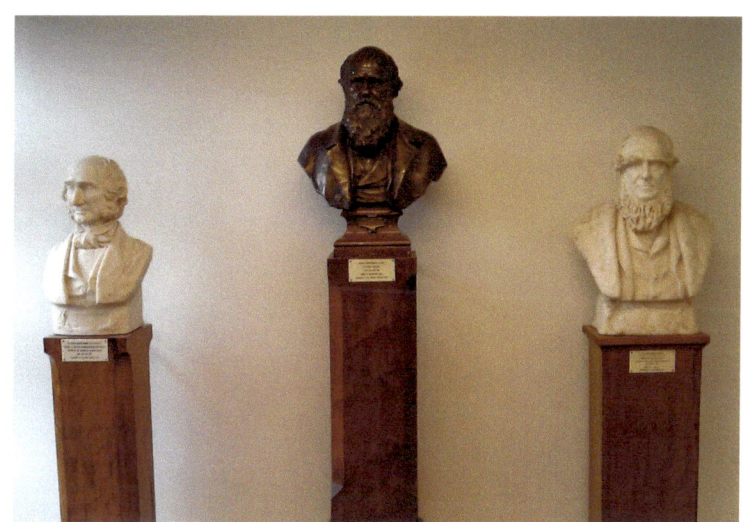

Sir William Jackson Hooker (centre), resident of Magdalen Street.

Willet, George Middleton, William Clabburn, L. E. Willett, the company floated under the Companies' Act 1856. William Clabburn went on to be a sheriff in 1866–67 and served on the jury of the Paris Exhibition. A later director was John Ayris who died in 1902. He was also a manager of the Norwich Waterworks Company, the Lowestoft and Yarmouth Waterworks Company, the Southern Waterworks Company and the Sheffield Company.

Prudence Blosse, wife of Thomas, mayor in 1612, left a house at Botolph Street as almshouses for widows. Botanist Sir William Jackson Hooker lived at Magdalen Street and James and Harriet Martineau and Elizabeth Fry were also born at Magdalen Street.

John Thirtle of the Norwich School of Artists was born in Norwich in 1777, and by 1800, after an apprenticeship, he established himself as printmaker and framer here in Magdalen Street. Having married the sister-in-law of John Sell Cotman, he later went on to become the president of the Norwich School of Artists in 1814.

William Boswell Jr (1840–89) was an ironmonger and photographer. His father, William Boswell, founded a company at No. 26 Magdalen Street.

Established in 1677, Doughty's Hospital appears not to have changed much and looks like a typical sheltered housing accommodation until the history of the hospital and building is delved into.

A mariner named William Doughty informed the Court of the Mayoralty that he wished to reside in Norwich and that he wished to be allowed to remain free of all taxes and charges, and in consideration of the favour he undertook to establish a hospital or almshouse in the city.

By 1687, he wrote a very long and complex will concerning the provisions:

1) He would leave a sum of £6,000 to his Trustees to be used for the purchase of a piece of land upon which the hospital would be built;
2) That land may not have been previously belonged to the Church;

3) He specified the building materials for the Hospital and the form it would take;
4) The building should cost no more than £600, with the balance being used to purchase land and tenements in Norfolk not '*subject to be overflowne with the sea*' to produce an income of at least £250, for the provisions of pensions and building repairs;
5) The Hospital would accommodate 24 poor aged men and 8 poor aged women, each to have a pension of 2/- every Saturday morning for food. They were to be provided with coal and a coat or gown of purple cloth, renewed every two years;
6) The Trustees should appoint a sober, discreet single man as Master, to dwell constantly in the Hospital and to see its well governing. The Master would receive 4/- a week for his pains;
7) Six years after the testator's death, or earlier if they were ready, the Trustees would convey the Almshouses, Lands and Properties to the Mayor, Sheriffs and Citizens of Norwich.

Early admissions included weavers, cordwainers, barbers, bakers, carpenters and tailors. In April 1700, the master, William Sydner, made a complaint regarding seven residents for 'miscarriages and misbehaviour'. The seven were produced at the Mayor's Court with one using 'opprobrious' words to the mayor. One apologised and was allowed to remain at the Hospital with the other six discharged.

Schoolmaster Blyth Hancock was admitted in 1791. He was educated in mathematical and scientific matters and two of his books were of astronomical calculations, and he was involved with the United Friars Society, which was formed in Norwich.

June 1835 saw the author Elizabeth Bentley admitted and was said to be one of the last people admitted under the old Court of Mayoralty. She died at the hospital aged seventy-two in 1839.

By 1810, the French wars had seen the hospital struggle, so a cash injection of £6,600 bequeathed by Thomas Cooke of Pentonville came in very handy. In November 1833, two of the king's Corporation Commissioners came to Norwich to receive evidence from the Court of the Mayoralty as to the finance of the many municipal city charities. The investigations led to the forming of the Municipal Corporations Act of 1835 and to changes in local government, and by August 1836, control of the Hospital along with other municipal charities were passed to trustees that were appointed by the Lord Chancellor.

Today all residents should be at least sixty and have lived in the boundaries of Norwich for a minimum of four years and be in financial need. The hospital is in the ownership of the Norwich Consolidated Charities and governed by a group of trustees.

N

Norwich Lanes

Norwich Lanes won the city category of GB High Street award for 2014. The area is of great historical interest and sits adjacent to the main city centre. The area is predominately pedestrianised, and the lanes are a series of alleyways, courtyards and open spaces and home to some of the most creative, independent retailers, eateries and pubs to be found in the UK.

With as many as 300 independent retailers, you will always find that something special that you are looking for. The year 2014 saw the Norwich Sound & Vision Festival, the inaugural Norwich Cocktail Week and the popular Norwich Lanes Summer Fayre, which can attract up to 15,000 people each year. Also in the lanes, you will find medieval churches, independent art galleries and two museums.

Dove Street was originally called Holdtor Lane. It was renamed Dove Street after the Dove Public House, which was formely the Edinburgh Arms. The street itself was the only main exit from the market. Although there were several lanes, Dove Street was the only exit where you could get a cart through, importantly if you were a market trader. When Queen Elizabeth I came to Norwich in 1578 to visit the Duke of Norfolk whose palace was at the bottom of Dove Street, she and her courtiers would have come down Dove Street.

Where Tesco stands used to be Chamberlin's Department Store. Mr Chamberlin arrived in Norwich in 1814, and by 1815 he had opened up his drapers' shop. By 1869 it was a department store. Chamberlin's closed down in 1963.

There is only one ironmonger left in Norwich, Thorns, which was established in 1835. Ironmongery had been present in Norwich since the days of the Normans. During the 1860s, a pastry shop caught fire and although not a big fire, the nearby ironmongers called Cubits had to wrap 400 lbs of gunpowder in wet cloth and move it to a safe house to avoid it exploding.

Another fire in the area took place in August 1880 at Herns the rope makers, and the fire spread to Chamberlin's and to the Norfolk and Norwich Subscription Library, where over 60,000 books were destroyed.

Lower Goat Lane took its name from the Old Goat Pub. The Grosvenor Fish Bar is a seventeenth-century timber-framed building with a medieval undercroft.

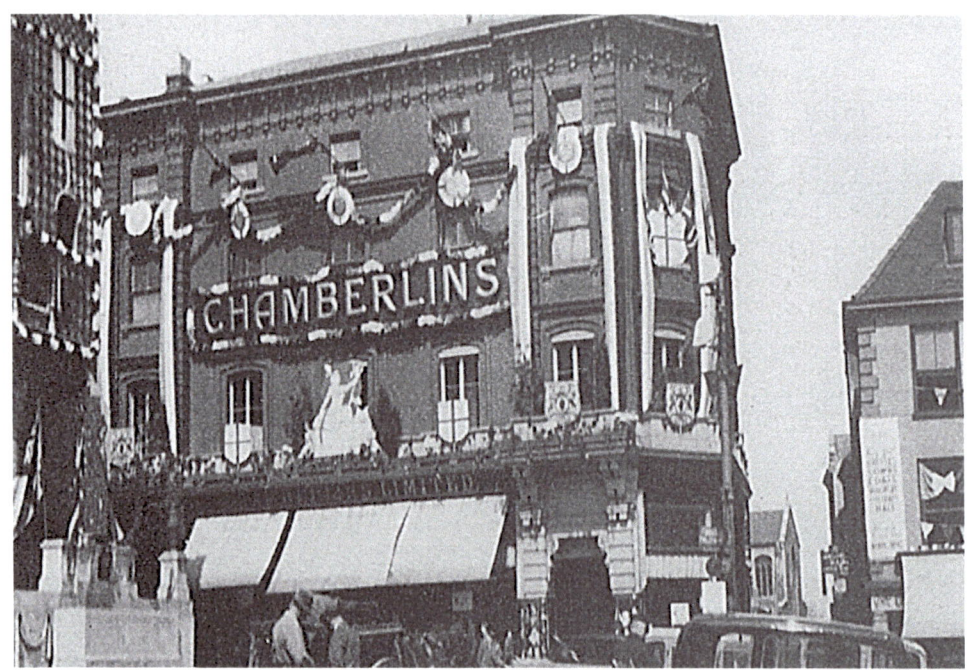

Above: Chamberlin's.

Below: Norwich Lanes.

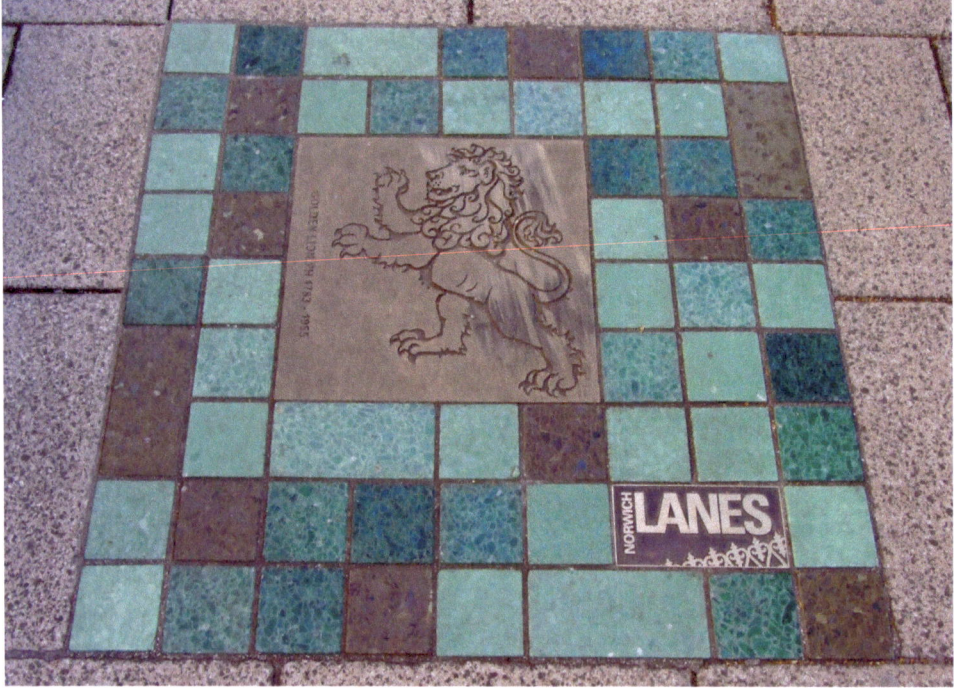

Oak Street

Houses, shops, courts and yards were demolished in the 1920s to make space for the new Sexton and Everard Shoe factory, which was built between St Mary's Plain and St Martin-at-Oak. The properties that were demolished were slums, and more damage had been done during the 1912 floods. The Great Hall had outbuildings and gardens. During the First World War, Flower Pot Yard was all but destroyed. Once described as the worst slum in Norwich, it was purchased by S. E. Glendenning who held it for twenty-five years to later demonstrate that the old houses of the area could be reconditioned, even after years of neglect. The Yard took its name from the Flower Pot Public House.

After S. E. Glendenning died, the Great Hall was sold to the Norfolk Archaeological Trust and then converted into office space.

The *Press* of 30 June 1851 reported that a murder was discovered in the area. The killing had taken place fifteen days earlier, but it was not solved until 1869. The *Press* stated that a body had been hacked into pieces and spread the parts across the city.

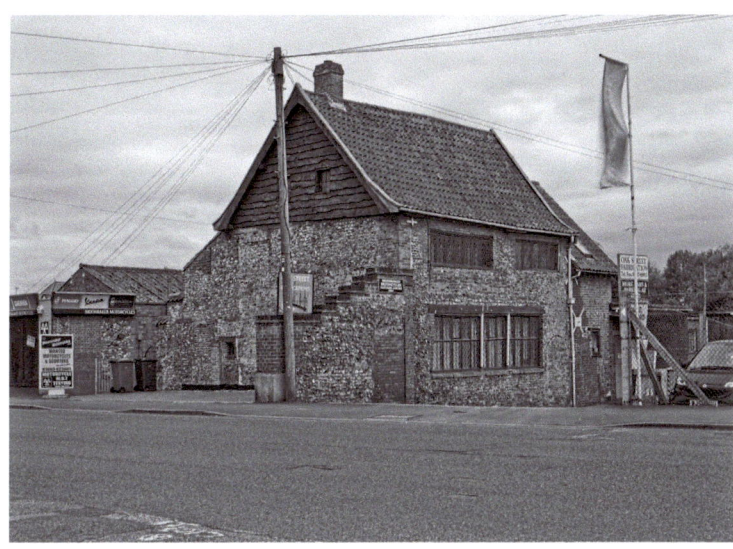

Great Hall.

The police dragged the river, taking in Trowse to Lakenham, but nothing of any significance was found.

In June, the city sewer cleaner found more parts of a body, and they were sent to the Guildhall where the picture was being put together. Publican William Sheward had told everyone that his first wife Martha had left him to go abroad in 1851. Over the years, William moved to different public houses, before becoming a pawnbroker. By 1868, he was the landlord of the Key & Castle pub at 105 Oak Street. He had since remarried and was suffering from bouts of depression. He thought that a visit to his sister in London would help. On 1 January 1869, he visited Walworth Police Station and told Inspector Davis that he had murdered his wife Martha in Norwich many years ago. He also said that he had a razor and was going to take his own life; he gave the razor to the inspector and made a full statement saying that they lived in Ber Street as the licensee of the Rose Tavern. He had had many failed businesses and was declared bankrupt in 1849.

He was taken back to Norwich on 7 January where he was charged with murder. He stated that he slit his wife's throat and cut up the body and disposed of it all around the city.

Sheward became the first private execution in the city with over 2,000 waiting outside the prison.

Just by Talbot Square lies the old Hebrew Congregation Cemetery. Although it is situated in the Church of England parish of St Michael at Oak, it was cut-off with the construction of the Inner Ring Road and now it fits in with the St Augustine's area. The cemetery was purchased in the names of Barnett Crawcour, Henry Carr, Israel Jacobs and Colman Michael. In the early days, the coffins were taken down a narrow path from St Martin's Lane, now Quaker Lane, and in its forty years of use there were only thirty interments here. The reason for this was that in 1854 the new Burial Act forbade burials to take place in churchyards and cemeteries within the city walls, and in 1856, a Jewish plot was made available at the cemetery situated at Bowthorpe Road. Barnett Crawcour is buried there along with Elm Hill Jeweller Simon Aaron, and the city's Kosher butcher Lyon Mordecai.

Sexton, Son & Everard shoe manufactory was founded in 1886 by Henry Sexton, and he was later joined by his five sons Henry, Jessie, Arthur, Fred and Alfred. Henry Senior along with three of his sons worked for Howlett and White, and when Henry set up in business, it was George White who gave him his first order.

Henry died in 1897, and by the start of the century, the company employed over 900 people. In 1916, a new factory was built on what was known as St Mary's Works. In 1921, a newer factory was built on the opposite side giving over 120,000 square feet. By the Second World War, the company employed 1,700, and during this time the factory was hit by enemy bombing, but the company continued and also was involved with government service contracts.

After the war, another factory was built on the site of St Mary's Plain. Their own label was later sold to Lilley and Skinner and Saxone who were later absorbed into the British Shoe Corporation.

The company then started to produce shoes for Marks & Spencer. The company later lost the contract due to being undercut on costs. In 1969, the company became part of the John James Group of companies, but within four years the receivers were brought in and on Wednesday 30 February 1972, 700 employees received their notices. By March, property developer Jack Taubman managed to negotiate an agreement that all assets would be transferred to a new company called Sexton Shoes Ltd. By 1976, there was 240 staff and 6,000 pairs of shoes were being produced each week, but the board called in the receivers. St Mary's has now been converted into individual units.

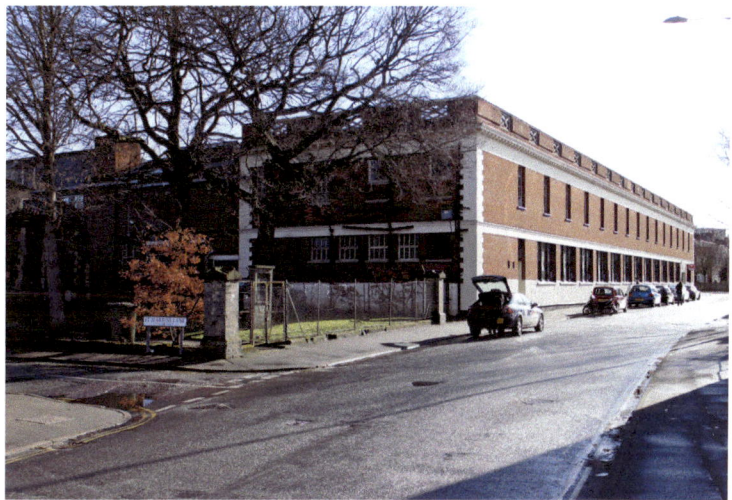

Sexton Son & Everard Ltd, who specialised in gents' dancing shoes and girls' dancing sandals.

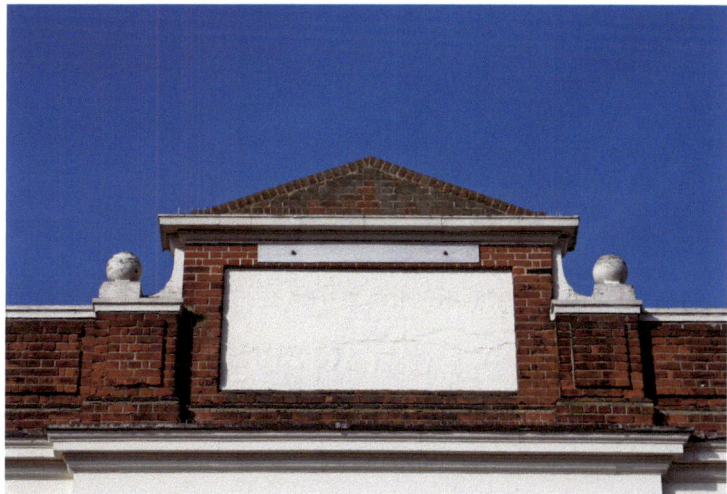

Sexton Son & Everard Ltd closed for good in 1976.

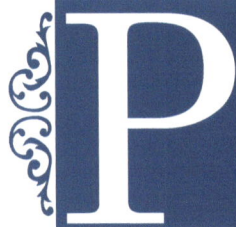

Peter Mancroft

This parish started at the beginning of the reign of Edward the Confessor, and towards the end of his reign, it was built over and inhabited. By 1086, the field was owned by Ralf de Guader, Earl of Norfolk.

After the church had been left in a poor state, the Dean and Chapter of St Mary's decided to rebuild it in around 1390, but it was not until 1430 that the first stone was laid with the help of gifts and legacies from wealthy citizens, and the church was consecrated twenty-five years later.

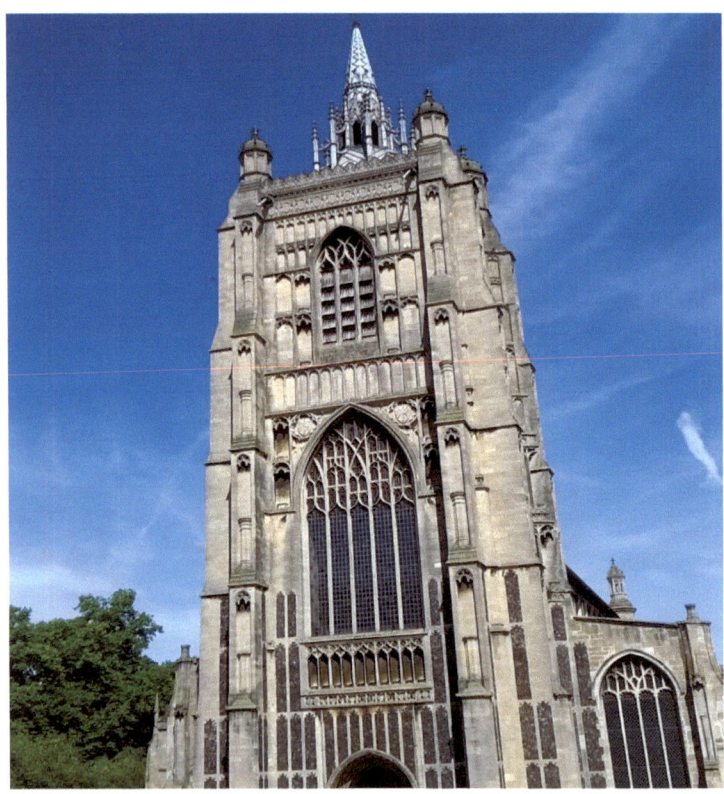

St Peter Mancroft.

The church was originally dedicated to St Peter and St Paul and then just St Peter, and it is possible that the word Mancroft comes from the old English word 'Gemæne Croft' (Common Field) or from the Latin '*Magna Crofta*' (Great Field). It has even been suggested that it might even have been named after the owner of the land whose name was Mann or Manne.

The nave is 60 feet tall with eight arched bays and a continuous clerestory of seventeen windows on each side.

When John Wesley visited Norwich he wrote in his diary:

I scarcely remember ever to have seen a more beautiful parish church; the more so beautiful its beauty results not from being ornaments, but from the very fine form and structure of it. It is very large, and of uncommon height, and the sides are almost all window; so that it has an awful and venerable look, and at the same time surprisingly cheerful.

In England's *Thousand Best Churches*, Simon Jenkins wrote:

Few who enter St Peter's for the first time can stifle a gasp. The sense of space and light is overwhelming. To those who find Perpendicular bland or lacking in shadow or mystery. Norwich answers with a blaze of daylight, as if the sky itself had been invited to pray.

St Peter Mancroft courtyard.

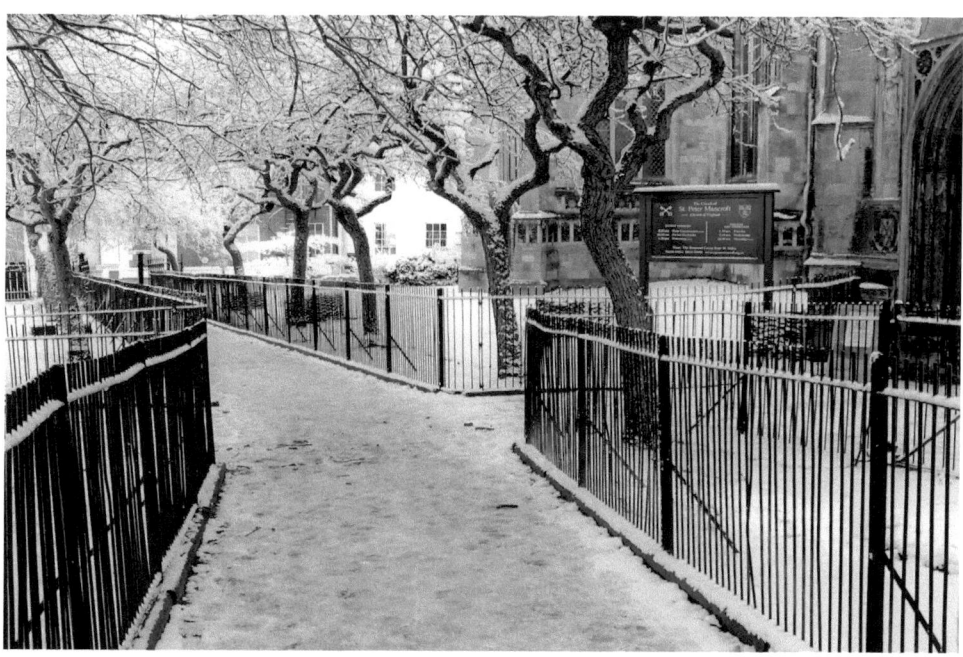

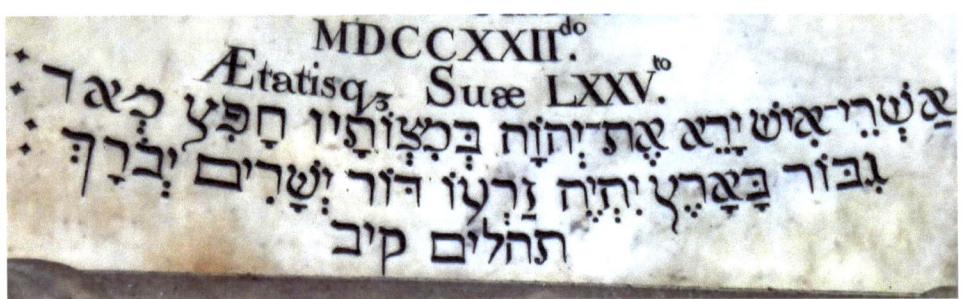

Plaque in Hebrew for historian John Mackerell.

The St Anne Chapel on the south aisle was where mothers and daughters once met who were members of the medieval Guild of St Anne, which was a forerunner to today's Mother's Union.

The church also possesses one of the five remaining parts of parochial libraries in Norfolk. In all, there are sixteen books that date from the twelfth century to the year 1763, which include a manuscript Vulgate of 1340.

The Octagon was built in 1983 costing £250,000 and it was derived from the common medieval plan of octagonal chapter houses attached to medieval cathedrals.

An unusual in St Peter Mancroft is one dedicated to a Mr Knott:

> Here lies a man who was Knott born
> His father was Knott before him.
> He lives Knott, and he did Knott die,
> Yet underneath this stone doth lie.
> Knott christened, Knott before.
> And here lies, and yet was Knott.

John Grix was a chorister and a leader of the scouts group that was attached to the church. Aged fifteen, he lied about his age to become a member of the Civil Defence. He rode his bike when air-raid sirens were sounded, and he took messages to the fireman on duty. On one occasion, he helped rescuers to help those hurt. He was sprayed with acid but kept on helping out. He believed he was only doing what was expected of him, and he was amazed when the post brought the news that he was to receive the British Empire Medal for his bravery. When George V came to the city, John was brought to his attention, and the king commented, 'I understand you are only fifteen.'

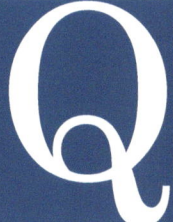

Queen Street

Queen Street is a thoroughfare from Bank Plain and the junction of London Street and St Andrews Street down to Tombland and Upper King Street.

St Mary the Less is situated here, and it was once leased to the city by the Dean and Chapter at the time of the Reformation for an annual rent of 4*d* for 500 years. It was later used as a hall for selling yarn, and by 1637, it was leased by the city to the French and Walloons.

Number 1 was once a late seventeenth-century house, and it is now used as a public house and has been listed as a Grade II building as it has a fifteenth-century undercroft, which shows that it had been under the ownership of the wealthy mercantile class over several centuries.

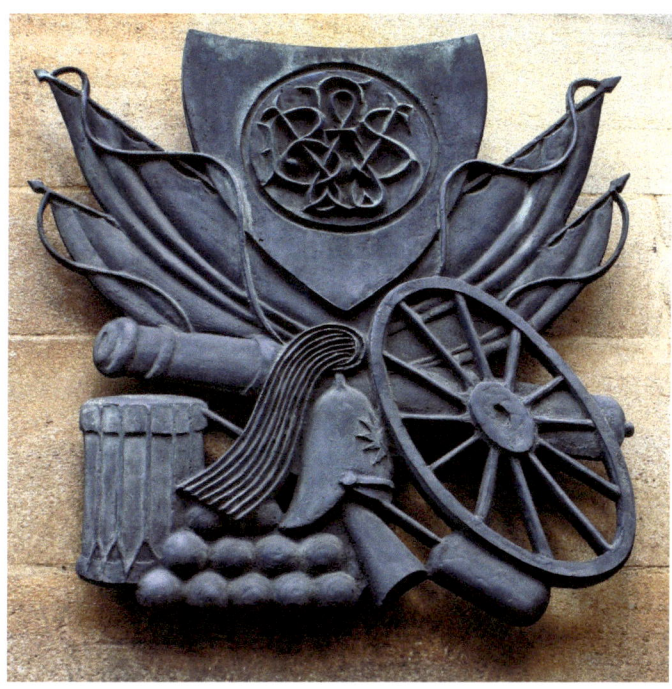

Queen Street.

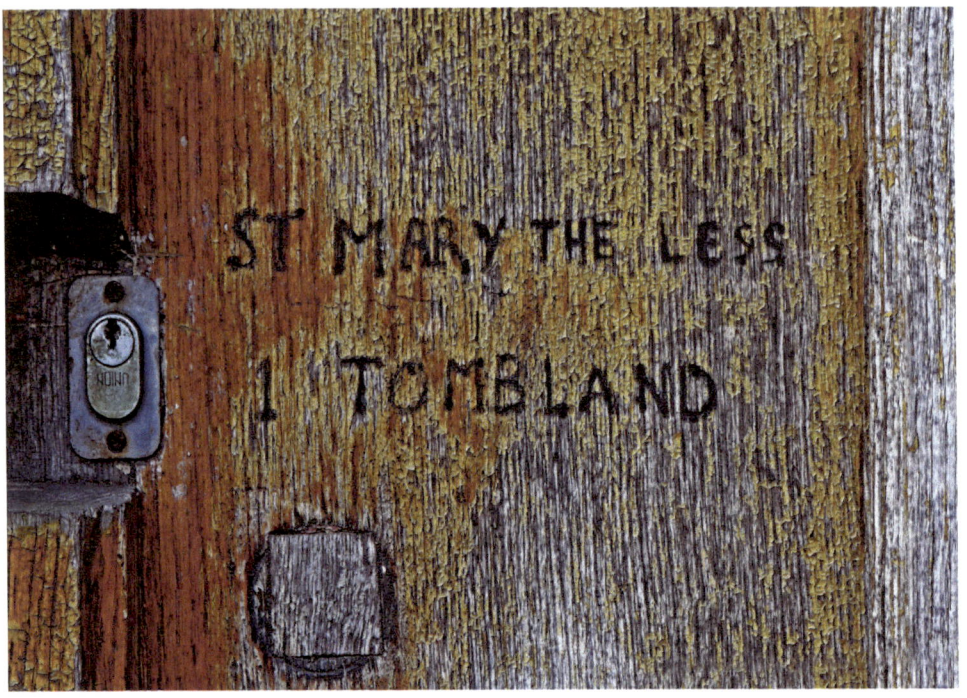

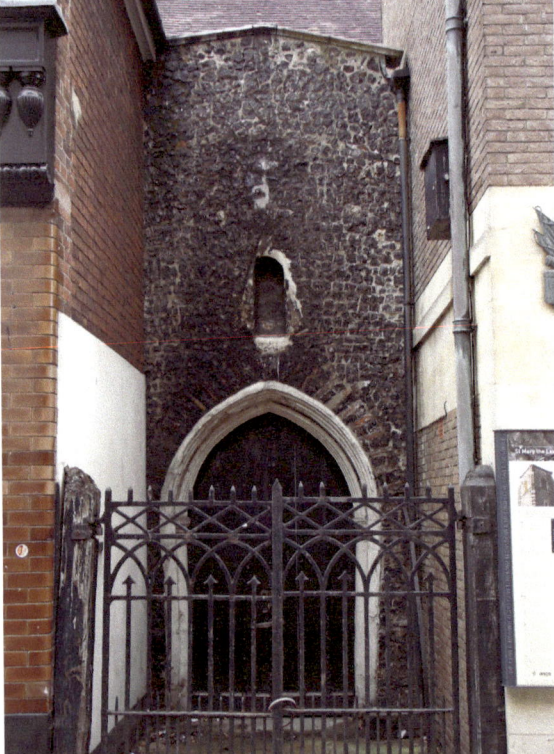

Above: St Mary The Less etched door.

Left: St Mary The Less.

Old Bank of England Court was the house of the earls of Buckingham. In 1810, Sir Lambert Blackwell of Easton, for a wager drove a coach, four in hand, into the yard, turned it round and drove it out again with 2 inches to spare. The name came from a branch of the Bank of England set up in 1828, but it was closed down on 31 May 1852. It was also the office to Norwich-born architect Edward Boardman (1833–1910), who alongside rival George Skipper went on to produce many buildings that still stand today. Edward was trained in London by the Lucas Brothers until he was articled with Lowestoft architect John Louth Clemence. He became a Fellow of the Royal Institute of British Architects (FRIBA) and moved to Old Bank of England Court in 1875. His most famous of works was turning Norwich Castle from a prison into a museum. He was elected mayor for 1905–06. He retired in 1933 and the business continued to 1966, and he is buried in the Rosary Cemetery.

P. Haldinstein and Sons

David Soman came from France to England during the late eighteenth century. In 1846, Philip Haldinstein married a daughter of Soman and became a partner in his shoe business. By 1853, the business was dissolved and then carried on by Philip, who brought his son Woolfe into the partnership in 1870. The business was then taken over by Philip's second son Alfred and with his two sons Henry W. Haldinstein and Geoffrey P. C. Haldinstein. Alfred was the first member of the family to enter public life. He acted as sheriff in 1897 along with being the Commissioner of the Peace (JP).

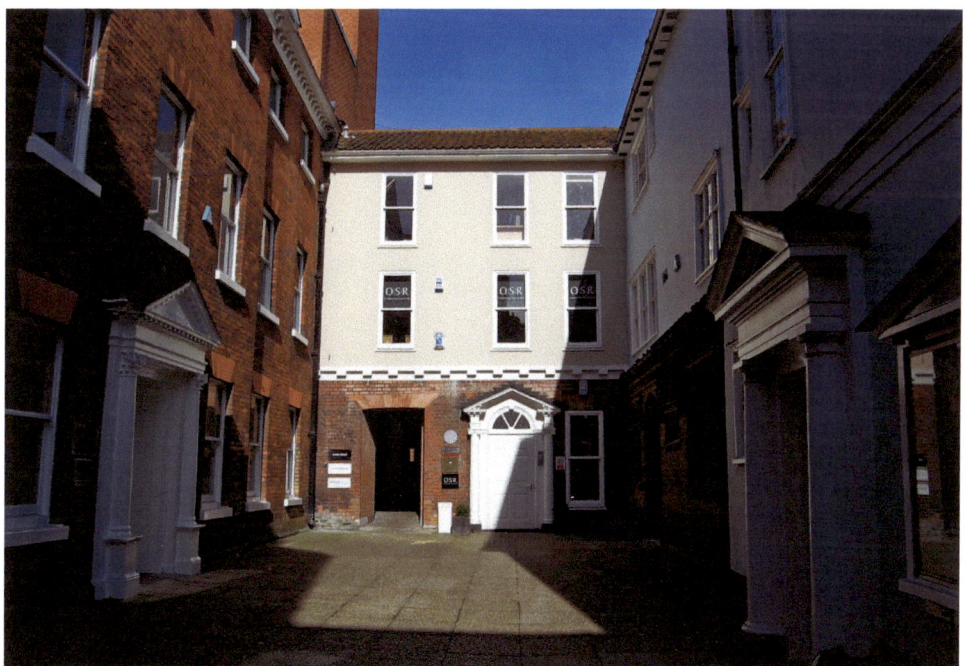

Old Bank of England Court.

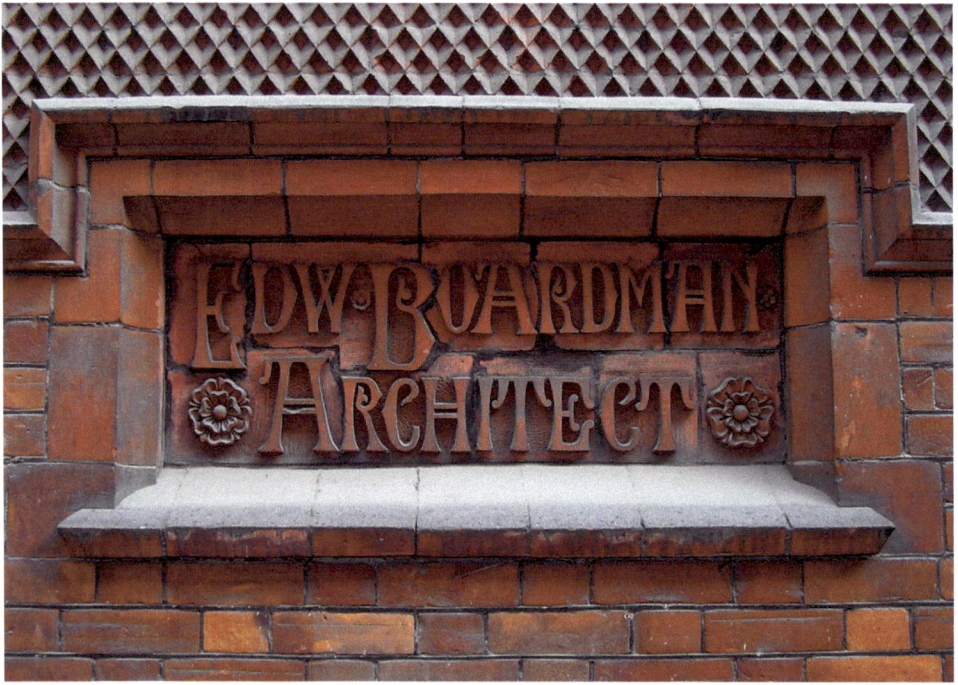

Edward Boardman.

Mrs Haldinstein gave cookery lessons for the education authority. Alfred was also the president of the Jewish Congregation Synagogue for over fifteen years.

The company expanded with branches in London, Leicester, Norwich, Kettering and Wymondham. The original Norwich building adjoins the warehouse, which had four floors with office and sample rooms. On the first floor, there would be up to one hundred clickers at a time. In all, at Norwich, there were seven blocks of buildings that ran from Queen Street through to Princes Street and then bounded by Redwell Street, and by the churchyard of St Michael at Plea was a warehouse with five floors. P. Haldinstein and Sons went on to become Bally Shoes.

Edward Boardman and Sons, architects and surveyors, were one of the oldest firms of that trade in the city. It was set up in 1860 by Alderman Edward Boardman, having learnt his trade from Messrs. Lucas Brothers, from where he was in charge of the restoration of Somerleyton Hall. Edward T. Boardman joined the firm in 1899, and in 1900, Edward Boardman retired.

Robert Ferror, mayor in 1526 and 1536, lived with his family at No. 3 and was a wool trader. In 1789, brewer Charles Weston was registered as living at No. 4.

R

Royal Arcade

This wonderful arcade was opened in 1899 and is 247 feet long. Built by Dereham-born George John Skipper in an art nouveau design, it also featured motifs such as floral shapes and peacocks on tiles that were designed by W. J. Neatby and manufactured by Doulton. A restoration took place in the 1980s. Skipper was educated at Bracondale School, and later he attended Norwich School of Art. He undertook training in London before returning to Norwich to work for his father.

Sir John Benjamin considered that, 'He was to Norwich what Gaudi was to Barcelona.'

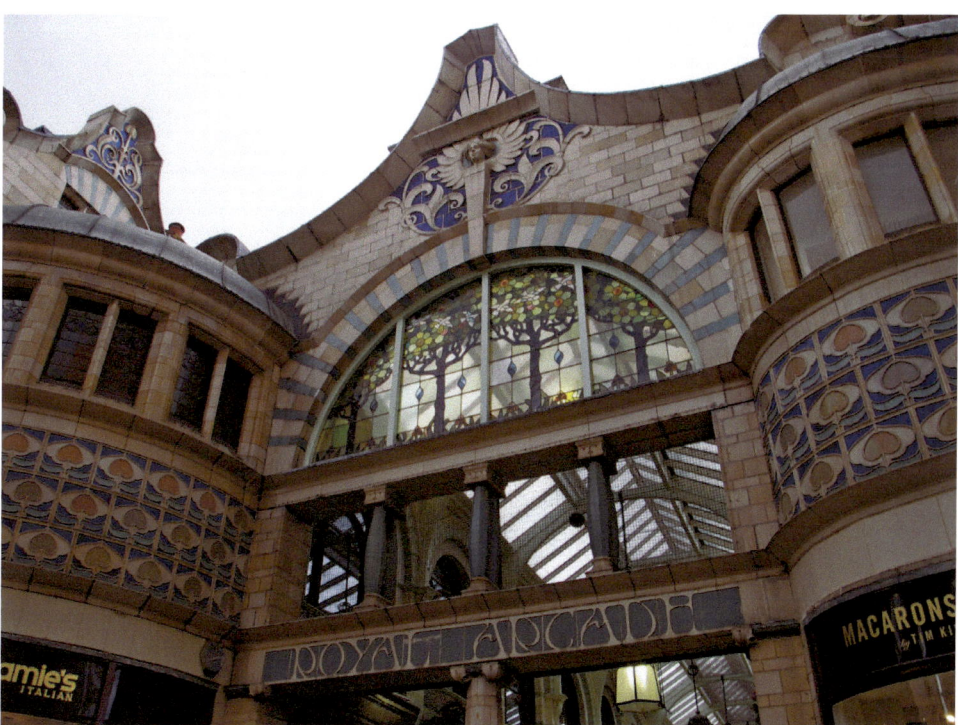

Royal Arcade.

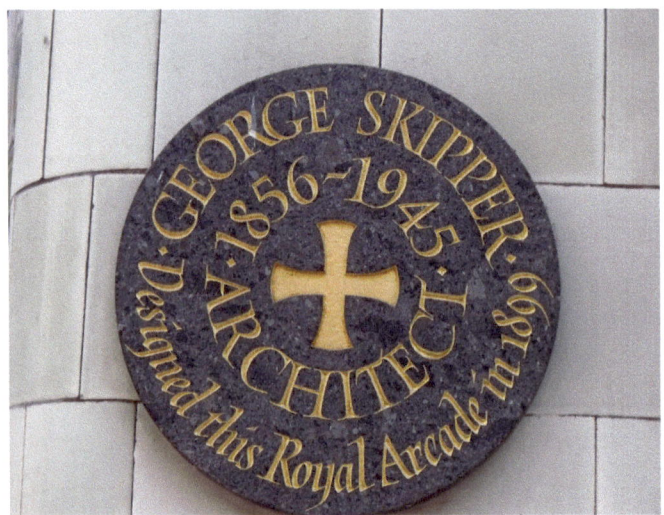

George Skipper plaque.

From the fifteenth century, the site was the Angel public house, which was renowned for the travelling shows that it hosted. Elephants were shown to the people of Norwich in 1685 and also the public house showed freaks and curiosities of the day.

By the 1830s, the Angel was the headquarters of the Norwich Whigs. A fight took place between the Whigs and the Tories, and the mayor had to read the Riot Act and to call on the military to restore order.

When the Angel closed, it became the Royal Hotel and stayed open for fifty years before being replaced by a bigger hotel at Prince of Wales Road.

Joseph Stannard was commissioned to rebuild the Gentleman's Walk entrance in 1846 and fifty years later the Royal Arcade housed twenty-four bow-fronted shops along with a pub and a clubroom. The original designs of the arcade clearly show that he was looking at ideas from art nouveau, which came from Samuel Bing's art shop Maison L'Art Nouveau.

On 24 May 1899, the opening of the shopping arcade was celebrated with justifiable civic pride.

Some of the other prestigious buildings that Skipper created in Norwich include his office that was above Jarrolds (1896); Norfolk Daily Standards Office in St Giles Street (1899–1900); Haymarket Chambers (1901–03); Norwich Union (AVIVA) headquarters in Surrey Street (1901–06); Commercial Chambers in Red Lion Street (1901–03); Jarrolds in Exchange Street and London Street (1903–05); Norfolk and London Accident Assurance Offices of 41–43 St Giles Street (1906), now a hotel; and the London and Provincial Bank (1907).

Sub-Leets

A sub-leet was a medieval legal administrative area and court, requiring various offices such as sheriff, treausrer, clerks, coroners and constables. The Anglo-Saxon settlement called Conesford survived despite the building of the castle and cathedral fees that was on land that housed townsmen. Another settlement, Westwyk, survived, but during the thirteenth century, the name was superseded by 'Wymer'. This name was also mentioned in the Domesday Book account of Norwich. Sub-divisions became documented in the thirteenth century, and it was decided that the boundaries of the sub-leets were made so that each contained up to twelve tithings, meaning that each would be represented by a jury of twelve Capital Pledges that were required by law to

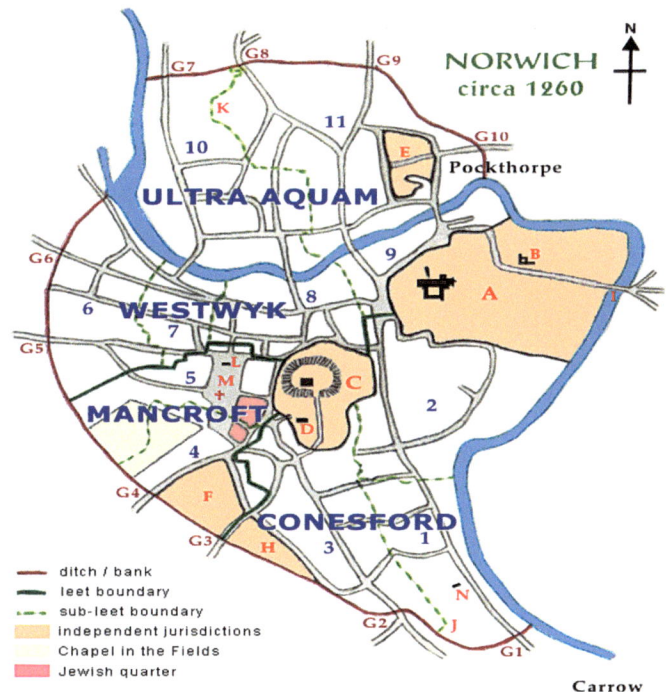

Sub-leets.

make presentment in the Leet Court. By the time of the late Middle Ages, the areas were moved by shifts in population.

By the last part of the fourteenth century, sub-divisions were treated in their own rights as leets and in the fifteenth century an electoral system was developed under the title of 'Great Wards'. These were later placed into three aldermanries, which were based on the original sub-leets.

Southern Conesford

This came from the time of the Norman Conquest. It housed rich citizens on the northern Conesford, and many private quays were placed on the riverside.

Northern Conesford

The two Conesford sub-leets came together by the mid-fourteenth century. The number of people was reduced, and large areas of land were later taken by the Augustinians and Franciscans for their precincts.

St Peter de Mancroft

Because this was on the marketplace, it became one of the most popular parishes in the city. The original church was in the ownership of the Earl who along with the king were the founders of the Newport. Rebuilt in the fifteenth century, its parishes were the city's richest merchants.

Berstrete

This was an Anglo-Saxon road.

Translation of Conesford, 8 February 1288, Berstrete Sub-Leet

Geoffrey de Howe harboured William de Stirston, who was not in tithing. William Calf in mercy for showing great contempt to the bailiffs by refusing to take oath; afterwards, he swore his oath. William de Denne had harboured Robert de Howe, son of Alexander de Brakendene, for two years. He is consequently in mercy because Robert was out of tithing. Robert de Mendham (sworn), William Godynow (sworn), Henry Pope (sworn), Geoffrey de Howe (discharged), Edmund de Stafford (sworn), Geoffrey fitz Baldwn (sworn), John de Ashill (sworn) Henry de Hoyland (sworn), Simon le Prude (sworn), Simon fitz Ranulph (sworn), Eudo de Tybenham (sworn), William Calf (sworn), Thomas le Neve (sworn), who present on their oath that John the servant of Robert Cann drew blood from Ralph de Aslakton baker.

They say that Beatrice la Qwyte and her associate Acilia habitually stole fleece from sheep and removed the fleece from the sheep of John Molle chaplain, and they stole a surcoat priced at 40d from the house of Henry Gylur; they carried off the fleeces and surcoat to the house of Geoffrey Munne, who knew about the felony and harboured them.

They say also that Richard Cokard is a thief and habitually steals geese and hens and has been a thief for seven years. Also they present Robert Scott and the husband of Emma le Hauteyn for the same. They also present that Beatrice, daughter of Robert Beumund, raised the hue, and it was pursued as far as the tollbooth. They present also that Henry de Caumbys is a thief, and they consider him suspicious, and that he acts contrary to the peace, and that he is well-dressed and no one knows by what means he can offer good clothes, and he is always wandering around at night.

They also present that the Prioress of Carrow and Robert Gerveys of Bracondale use the greenery in the city ditches as pasturage and have pigs and sheep there in the keeping of swineherds and shepherds. They also present that Thomas le Schowthere, residing by Trowse Bridge, buys grain before it reaches the market, with the result that etc. [i.e., the bailiffs lose the toll payable from the importer of the grain]. Roger de Clakeston for the same. Robert Gerveys of Bracondale for the same. Geoffrey Ringolf for the same.

They present that all brewers sell contrary to the assize. They also say that Adam de Barsham drew blood from Matilda le Ledbettere. Adam also drew blood from William, son of Richard de Gontorth. John Gylur drew blood from Geoffrey Munne. They say that all fisherman and poulterers have bought before the hour, etc. They also present that Vincent and Adam de saham dug up the highway at the Old Swinemarket. Nicholas de Reymerston made an encroachment 18 feet long and 3 inches wide. They also say that John de Ely linendraper sells beer for a penny.

They also say that Thomas Gerveys and Walter Hee have fuller's block for conducting fraudulent work on old clothes. They also present that Walter Hee has an unsealed measure so that those measures make a gallon (sic). They also say that Roger Burgeys broke down the door of Simon le Prude. They also say that John Qwyt, John Hert Senior of Trowse, Walter Hunne, Stephen le Carecter, John Croke, Walter Bely, and John Strike sell unwholesome meat. John Pekok baker drew blood from Ralph the servant of Richard de Aylesham at the bakery of Peter de Wyleby. They also say that the anchorite of All Saints has blocked up the Cockey so that no one can cross over it there.

They also say that Roger de Lakenham had sold Jewish meat known as *trephah*. They also say that Humphrey de Alderford drew blood from Alexander Cully with a cudgel and Alexander raised the hue. They also say that Ralph de Mangrene blocked the highway for 6 feet of its width opposite his stall, so that carts cannot get past there. Roger Beumund has an extremely unpleasant dunghill. William de Kesewyk for the same. Martin le Rede, lodging with Richard de Aylesham, is out of tithing. John Keye is out of tithing.

Roger, son of Richard de Aylesham, is out of tithing. Henry de Bekles chaplain raised the hue on William de Lakenham in the parish of St Martin. Marion, wife of Roger de Corston, raised the hue on Reginald de Lakenham in the same parish. Gundredale Puddingwyf raised the hue on William le Linite. Richard le Hemenhale raped Hawisia Balle. Hamon the smith of Trowse bought grain, with the result that the bailiffs, etc. The wife of Thomas le Cordewaner raised the hue on Reginald de Lakenham.

They say that the poulterers and fisherman (as above). They present also that the wife of Andrew Skeppere, who lodges in the house of William de Buretoft, is a thief and stole from the house of William de Lakenham butcher a surcoat priced at 12*d*. And she is habitually doing this kind of thing. They present also that Robert Scot habitually climbs over walls at night and breaks through walls [of houses] and carries out other felonies.

St Giles, St Margaret, St Swithin and St Benedict

This was known by its parishes. By the fourteenth century, the division was known by the district of St Giles.

St Lawrence and St Gregory

This was known by its parishes. By the fourteenth century, the division became known as St Gregory.

St John de Maddermarket, Holy Cross, St Andrew, St Michael de Motestow and St Peter

This was known by its parishes. By the fourteenth century, the division became known as St Andrew.

SS Simon and Jude, St George before the gates of the Holy Trinity and St Martin before the gates of the Bishop

This was known by its parishes. By the fourteenth century, the division became known as St George. The Wymer sub-leets were reduced to three.

St Michael de Coselanye, St George, St Mary and St Martin

This was known by its parishes. By the fourteenth century, the division became known as St Michael.

St Olave, St Botulph, St Clement, St Mary Combust, St Saviour, All Saints, St James, St Edmund the King and St Margaret Combust

This was known by its parishes. By the fourteenth century, the division became known as St Clement. The Two Ultra Aquam sub-leets became adjusted by the late fourteenth century in order to make three sub-divisions.

The presentment of offences in each of the sub-leet, by a twelve-men jury always started with a list of those selected to take the juror's oath that was then followed by the list of offences they reported.

Theatres

Opened in 1995 in a nineteenth-century maltings, Norwich Playhouse had been transformed into a fantastic performance space by Henry and Jane Burke. At various times, the building had been a builder's merchants, a Greek restaurant and a motorcycle dealership; it was also used as a munitions store during the Second World War. However, during its early years the theatre couldn't find an audience. In 1997, the future of the playhouse looked bleak

In early 1998, the new board decided to reopen as a receiving house. With input from Norwich City Council and the arts community of East Anglia, the Playhouse reopened in January 2000, with acts including Al Murray and the National Theatre on the bill. It was a huge success and showed a future was indeed possible for the theatre.

Under the leadership of Caroline Richardson, the theatre went from strength to strength, although the early 2000s were still difficult times for the venue. However, in 2004, Norwich Playhouse entered a management merger with Norwich Theatre Royal and received a grant from Arts Council England to repair and add facilities to the building, allowing rapid modernisation.

During the next few years, the theatre gained a reputation as an exceptional venue, and continues to work closely with promoters to attract new and better things to Norwich.

On 21 June 1737, parliament passed a Licensing Act that meant any actor who was performing without the king's patent or the licence of the Chamberlain would be performing illegally. These would only be issued for Westminster or wherever the king was. Twenty years later, the new theatre was built by Thomas Ivory who was the sole proprietor. The cost to build it was £600, and many lawyers and businessmen gave £20 through instalments.

Its first play on 31 January 1758 was *The Way of the World* by William Congreve. To get around the Licensing Act, Thomas renamed the theatre the Grand Concert Hall by Ivory.

On 8 March 1768, the theatre received the Royal assent and a licence was granted to Thomas Ivory who soon gave up his sole ownership by valuing the theatre at £6,000. Thomas divided the shares into thirty and kept two for himself.

Actresses Anne Brunton Merry and Sarah Siddons made their debuts between 1785 and 1788, and by 1801, the theatre was remodelled by Norwich architect William Wilkins. In the same year, a promising actress Sophia Ann Goddard died aged twenty-five. She was engaged to John Harrison Yallop, part of the Bolingbroke family, and she is buried in the Bolingbroke tomb in the graveyard of St Peter Mancroft.

In 1818, the actor Junius Brutus Booth appeared. His son John Wilkes Booth assassinated President Abraham Lincoln. In 1840, Liszt performed, and in 1842, nightly performances were introduced and for a short time the theatre was renamed Theatre Royal and Grand Amphitheatre of Arts. The theatres act was dropped, which allowed other theatres in the country to present dramas. In 1866, P. T. Barnum brought Mr and Mrs Stratton (Tom Thumb and his wife) to perform.

Charles Blondin (the Great Blondin) who crossed Niagara Falls by tightrope in 1856 played here in 1869. In 1915, two shows of variety and revue were shown, and the theatre for these shows were called Empire and Theatre Royal. By 1928, the theatre was owned by Joe Collins and Jack Goodwin.

In 1967, Norwich City Council purchased the theatre from owners Essoldo Cinemas for £90,000, and by 1968, parliament repealed the 1843 Theatre Act, abolishing the Lord Chamberlain's censorship. October 1990 saw Sir James Cleminson become the new Chairman of the Trust and was succeeded in 1998 by Jonathan Barclay.

In 2001, the thirteen-hour, nine-play Trojan war epic *Tantalus*, which was directed by Sir Peter Hall, was performed across three evenings. Norwich was one of the four tour venues to show it.

The Maddermarket Theatre opened in 1921 as the third home of the Norwich Players. The theatre was built as a Roman Catholic Chapel in 1794. It was also used as a grocery warehouse and a Salvation Army Hall. It has twice been extended in 1953 and 1966. A refurbishment took place in 2003.

Shropshire-born theatrical director and founder of the English Drama Society Walter Nugent Blight Monk (1878–1958) was invited to produce a show in St Andrew's Hall in 1909. The building cost Monk £1,700 and at least the same to convert it. The name came from the vegetable dye that was used in the Middle Ages. By 1933, the theatre became the first one in the world to have staged the whole collection of Shakespeare plays by one producer. Monk also took plays on the road, including plays about the black death of 1349, Kett's Rebellion of 1549 and the masque of Anne Boleyn, which was performed in the gardens of Blickling Hall in August 1938, with Queen Mary attending one of the performances.

After thirty-one years of service, Monk retired in 1952, but in 1948, he purchased a derelict building to the south and an appeal started to raise £25,000 for alterations, and in 1952, the Maddermarket Theatre Association, now the Friends of the Maddermarket, was formed. Completed in 1953, a gala matinee of Moliere's *Tartuffe* took place in front of the Queen Mother in 1954. Monk was awarded the CBE in June 1958, and when he died in October, Ian Emmerson became director, also serving for thirty-one years. In 1963, Ian launched the Youth Theatre Club, and he was also

T

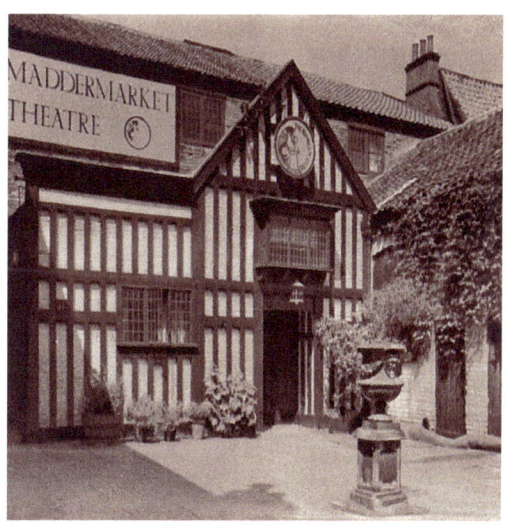

Maddermarket Theatre.

responsible in 1981 for the Tangent Theatre. Tangent produced up to five plays a season, but it became a strain financially and disbanded in 1986 when David Harris took over. Jane Rutherford took over in 1994 and then Andrew Kitchen in 1996 and Clare Goddard in 1999.

A ghost of a priest is said to have been seen by many in the theatre, including Monk, also, in Monk's day the cast were never named as he firmly believed that the play was more important.

Donald Pyle founded the Great Hall Theatre Company as a private theatre club in 1961. It was named after Pyle's own house, the Great Hall in Oak Street. The first performance starred members of the Conesford Players in the play *In the Round*. From 1964 to 1974, the company was resident at the Bakers' Arms in Heigham Street before moving to the Friend's Meeting House in Upper Goat Lane. By 1988, a move was made to St Peter's Hall in Park Lane before settling at the Assembly House in 2005.

Originally, the Sewell Barn Theatre was the barn of Clare House, which was owned by Philip Sewell who was a local benefactor and brother of Anna Sewell, author of the classic *Black Beauty*. When Philip died in 1906, he left the house and estate to the city of Norwich. Clare House became an Open Air School for city children who were suffering from respiratory complaints, and the barn became their washroom, restroom and handicraft centre.

The barn then went on to have many uses. During the First World War, it was used as a theatre where Catton residents put on concerts for troops that were billeted in the area. It then became a bicycle shed for the girls of the Blyth School, which was built on the grounds of Clare House in 1929. Demolished in 1970, it became part of the new Blyth Jex School, which is now Sewell Park College.

The theatre is the 'in-house' drama company of the Friends of the Sewell Barn, and became established by a series of workshops to bring young people and experienced

A–Z of Norwich

amateur actors along with directors and technicians within the city, and soon the intimate setting of the theatre was being developed.

The first artistic director was Henry Burke and his associate John Dane, a drama teacher at the neighbouring Blyth Jex School. In a short period of time, the established company was putting on challenging and ambitious plays.

The theatre seats around one hundred people on seating on three sides of an acting space, and in 2015, the theatre was honoured by the Norfolk Arts Award for their commitment to producing challenging productions.

Norwich Puppet Theatre (NPT) is based on the purpose-converted medieval church of St James'. The conversion work took place between 1978 and 1980, after a steering group set up by Ray DaSilva, Tony Ede and Linde Katritzky had found that the project was going to be viable. Ray and his wife Joan had run the DaSilva Puppet Company since 1962 – latterly in Godmanchester, Huntingdon – and had long held the dream of setting up a permanent base for their puppets. Tony Ede had first become attracted to puppetry as a Cambridge undergraduate when he visited the Salzburg Puppet Theatre, and Linde had been brought up on the continent to regard puppetry as a vital art form.

After looking at various churches under the care of Norwich Historic Churches Trust, their final choice was St James'. The starting point was an empty shell as St James' had become the night-shelter for Norwich after being declared redundant as a church. Then through a combination of fundraising, gaining support-in-kind, and using labour through the Manpower Services Commission scheme – which saw young apprentices working with professional craftsmen – the designs of local architect Peter Codling were brought into life.

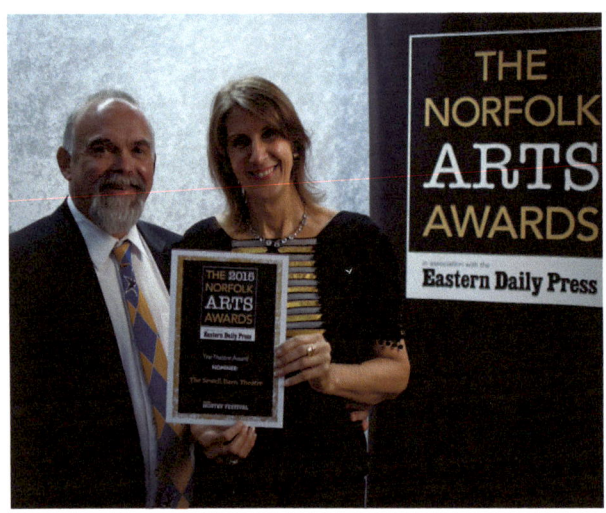
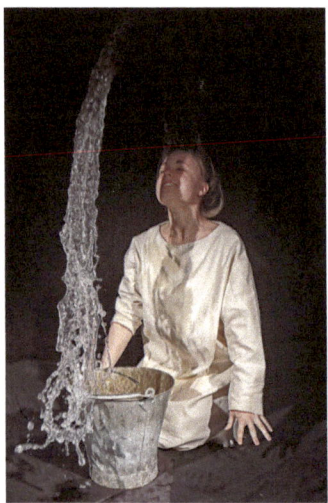

Above left: Sewell Barn Theatre Norfolk Arts Award.

Above right: Sewell Barn Theatre *Air Swimming*.

T

Opening on 1 December 1980, the former church now contained a 187-seat theatre – old cinema seats upholstered with bus seat fabric by two apprentices at City College – a stage with puppetry trench and marionette bridge, a foyer with shop and bar, and all the other facilities you'd expect. An excited audience were heralded by a Puppet Fanfare performed by Ray and Joan and then for that first Christmas performances of *Humbug* and *Pinocchio*.

Five years later, the Octagon Building opened that gave the theatre a second performance space as well as its own making workshop, administrative offices and gallery space. Norwich Puppet Theatre was then complete as you see it today.

In the thirty-five years since then, the Theatre has created shows under artistic directors Ray DaSilva, Barry Smith, Luis Boy and Joy Haynes ranging from traditional tales like Hansel & Gretel through to contemporary stories by Roald Dahl and Joyce Dunbar. Each play is created to be performed at the home base in Norwich and to be toured to other theatre venues across the country and schools in East Anglia. NPT also welcomes the best of British and international puppet theatre to its stage and provides the citizens of Norwich the range of experience that puppetry can offer.

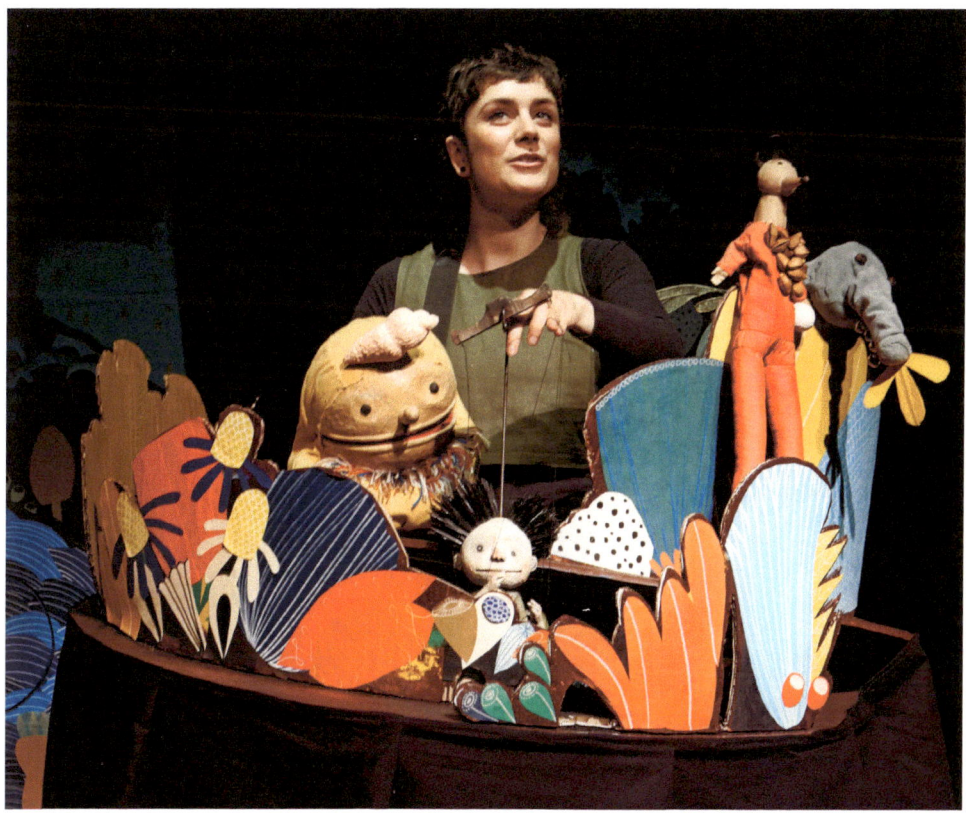

Norwich Puppet Theatre Andi Sapey.

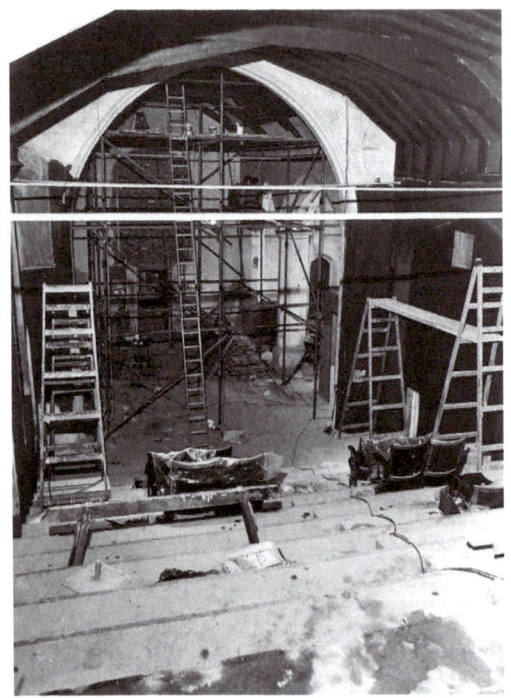
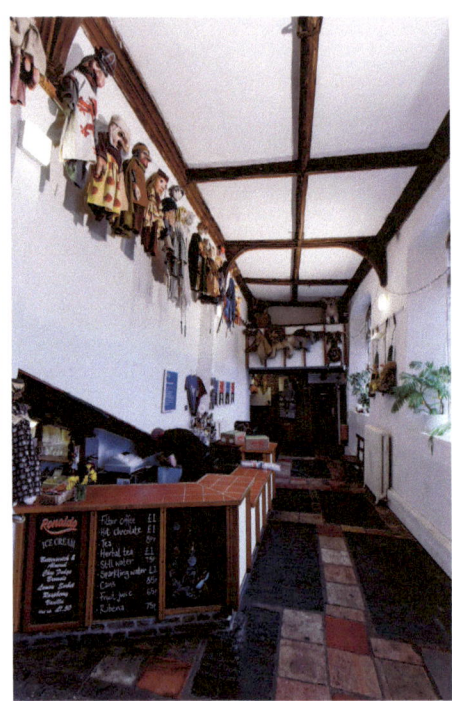

Above left: Norwich Puppet Theatre building work, January 1980.
Above right: Norwich Puppet Theatre foyer.
Below: Norwich Puppet Theatre evening foyer.

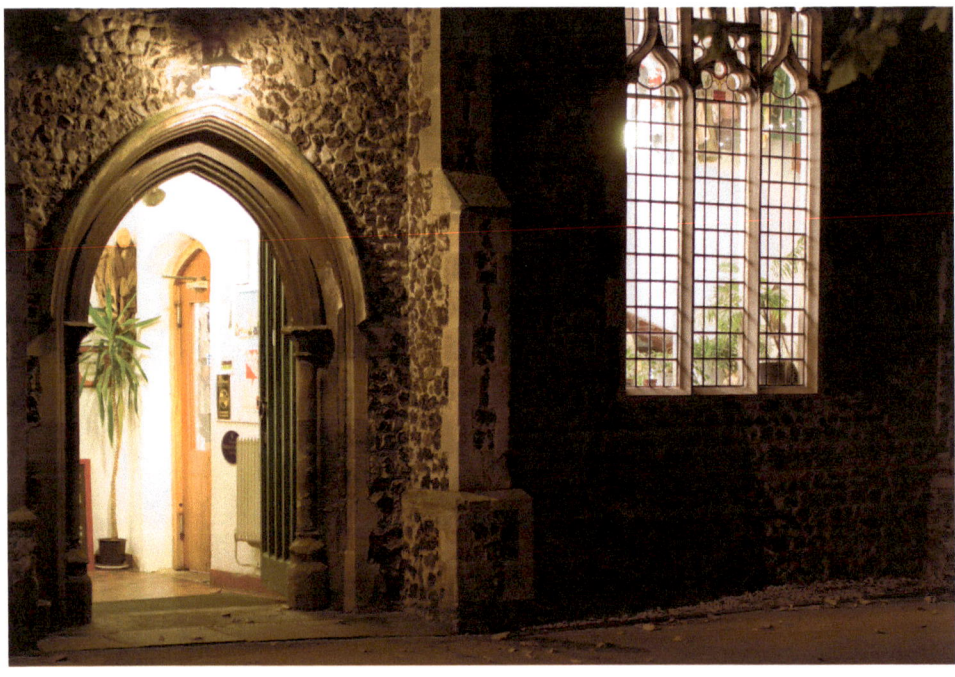

T

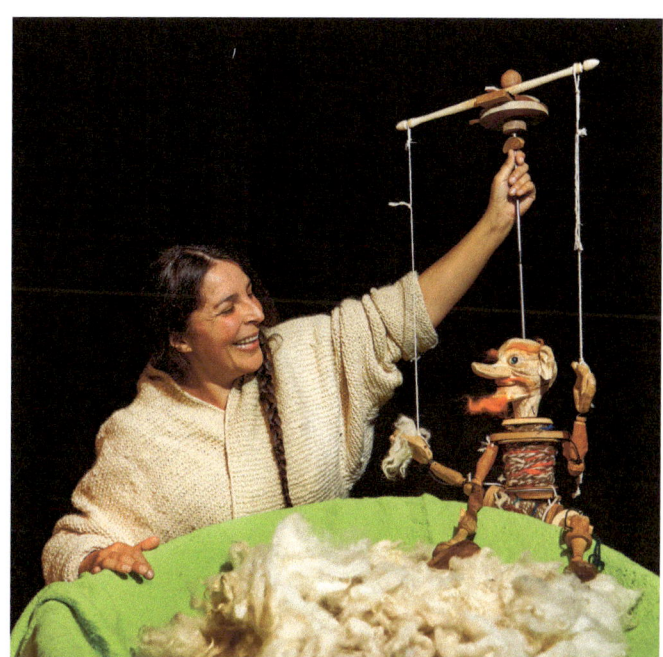

Norwich Puppet Theatre,
Rumpelstiltskin.

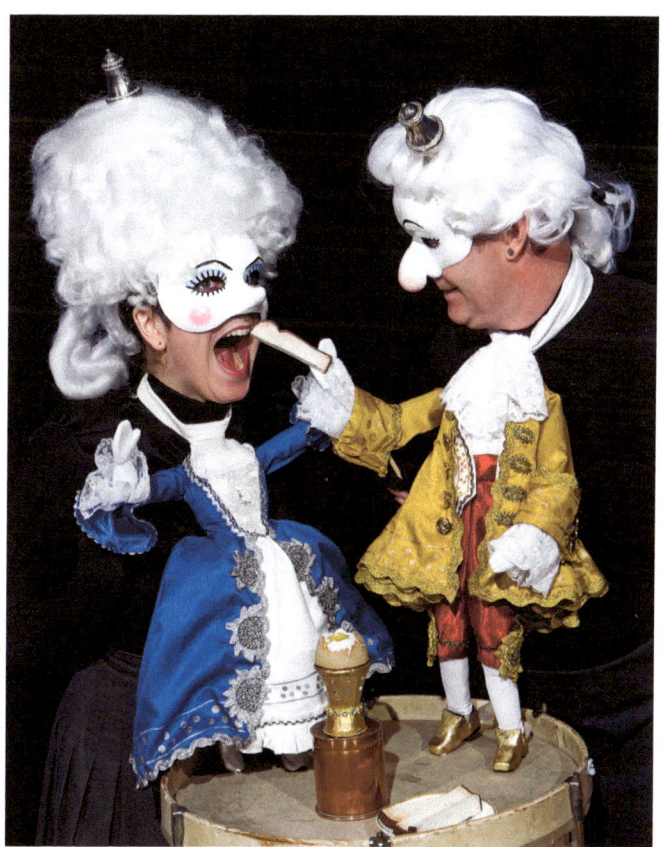

Norwich Puppet Theatre,
Tinderbox.

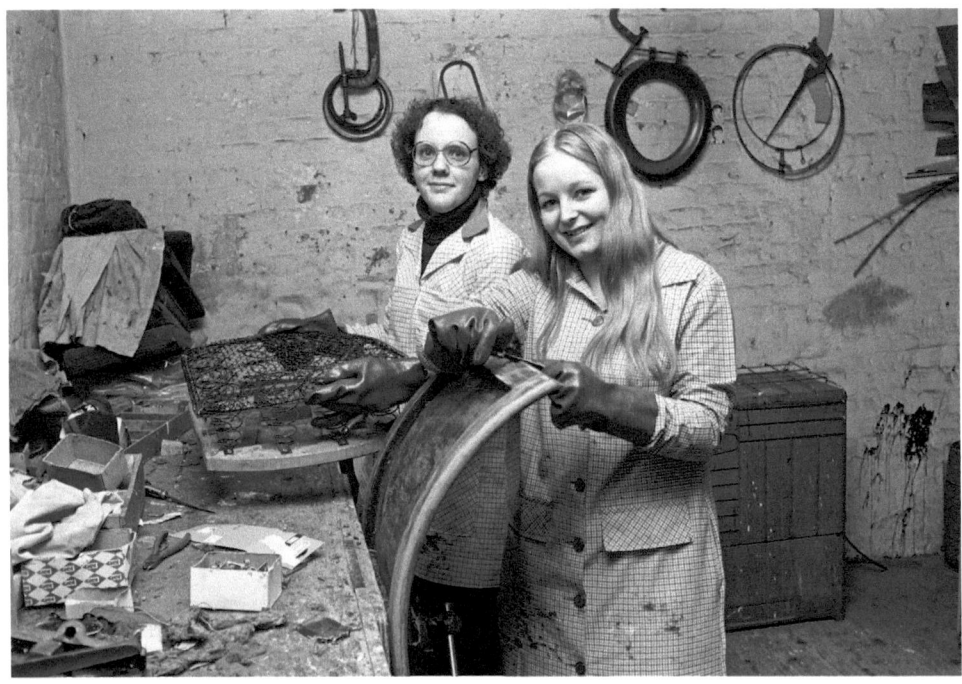

Above: Norwich Puppet Theatre upholstery taskers, 1979.

Left: Norwich Puppet Theatre work starts.

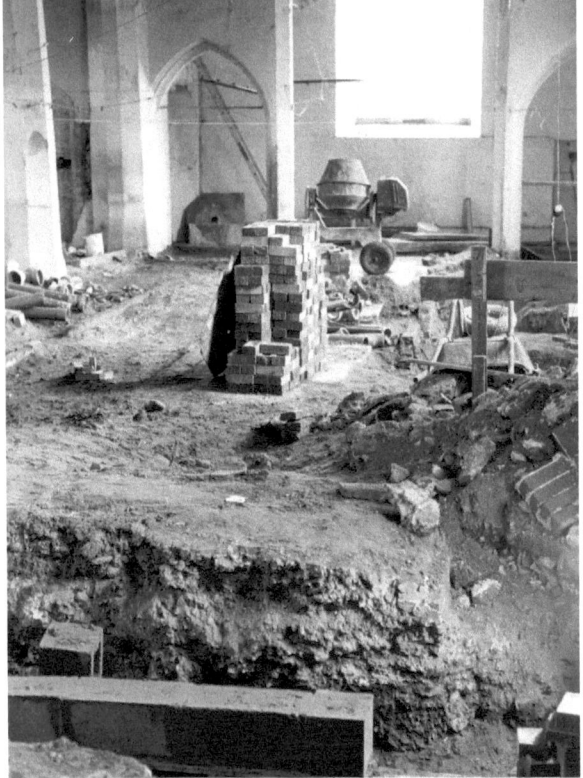

U

Underground

There are many tunnels underneath the fine city of Norwich, but it's hard to define their histories and separate fact from fiction. Some of the well-known tunnels include the following:

> The castle to the Guildhall and then on to Carrow Priory, which formed part of the old Colman's works at Bracondale and then on to the cathedral.
> The cathedral to nearby Samson and Hercules in Tombland to Princes Street and then to St Benet's Abbey at Ludham, although this part could be seen as a myth.
> Upper King Street to Pull's Ferry.
> The Prince's Inn situated in Princes Street to St Andrew's Hall.
> St Andrew's Hall to the Red Lion in St George's Street.
> Lower Goat Lane to St Giles Gate.
> The Shrub House in Charing Cross to St Benedict's Gate.
> The Mischief Tavern in Fye Bridge Street to St Clement's church.
> The Maid's Head Hotel to the Cathedral Close.
> The Pockthorpe Brewery in Barrack Street to Kett's Cave in Anchor Street.

One can only imagine what these tunnels were used for over the years, with many involving illegal activities.

As all of Norwich is underlain by chalk, it makes digging highly accessible. For many hundreds of years, chalk in Norwich was extracted for lime for construction use.

As well as tunnels for chalk mining, there have been many other openings, such as cellars, crypts and undercrofts. Some tunnels were used as shelters during the Second World War.

A tunnel at the cathedral is said to run for at least nine miles to the ruins of St Benet's Abbey, which is situated on the marshes at Ludham. Another tunnel from the cathedral was said to be used by monks to get to what is now known as Samson and Hercules House. The cathedral, or Blackfriars's Hall, is said to have a fifteenth-century tunnel leading to the corner of Redwell Street and Princes Street.

Augustine Steward House, having already been featured in this book, is said to have sixteenth-century passages. People have talked of a blocked tunnel leading to the cathedral and St Gregory's church.

The Missing Shoe in Castle Meadow that was once Pond's shoe shop is said to have two tunnels, one opposite to the castle and one north to Blackfriars Hall.

What was once the Princes Inn in Princes Street is said to have two tunnels, one leading to the cathedral and one leading to St Andrew's Hall, which was said to have been discovered near Elm Hill in the 1950s. It is also claimed that a blocked archway in the cellar at 29 Elm Hill housed a tunnel leading to the Briton's Arms. An undercroft in Wensum Street allowed people to move between the two streets for safety reasons possibly in the fifteenth century.

In what was once the Raven Pub in Lower Goat Lane, there is supposed to be a tunnel leading to what was St Giles Gate while monks are said to have used a tunnel from Charing Cross Street to what was St Benedict's Gate, and many tunnels can be found near Whitefriars Bridge and from Fye Bridge Street to St Clement's church.

There is said to be tunnels under the Maids Head Hotel as in 1644 Oliver Cromwell sent a group of men to Norwich to arrest a group of Royalists, and historically, it is claimed that the parliamentarians came to the hotel through a series of secret tunnels. Most of Cromwell's men were apparently beheaded in the tunnel.

The excavations have over the years suffered from subsidence and I'm sure that most people will remember when in 1988 at Earlham Road a double-decker bus fell into the earth. *The Evening News* went on to doctor the well-known picture showing a man with glasses in the hole with the caption 'Norwich's Lost Tribe'. The date of the newspaper was 1 April 1988. Cadbury's also used a photograph for its slogan 'Nothing fills a hole like a Double Decker'.

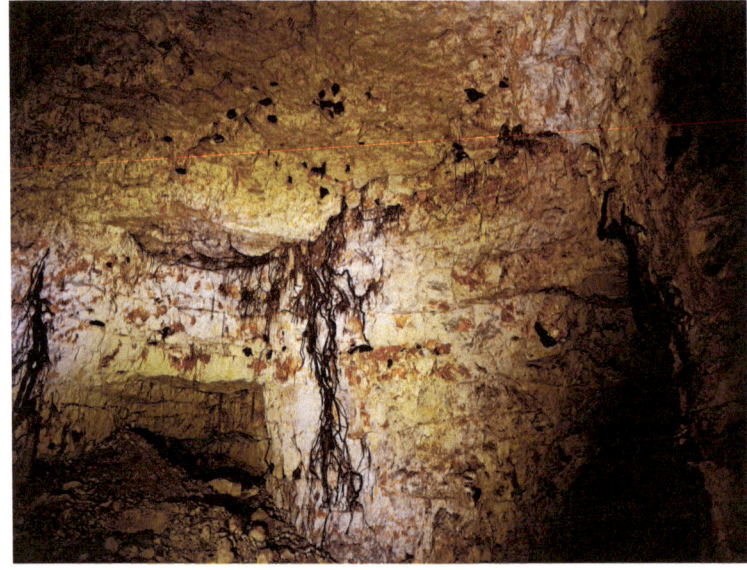

Rosary Road.

Victoria Station

Norwich's Victoria Station was once part of the original Eastern Union Line to Norwich, which opened in December 1849. It closed to passengers in 1916 and remained for coal and cement traffic. It was also the terminus of the Great Eastern Main Line. It was originally opened by the EUR (Eastern Union Railway) with passenger services in December 1849, and the booking hall once housed a circus known as Ranelagh Gardens that was run by Pablo Fanque. Some will remember the name as it was used in the song 'Being for the Benefit of Mr Kite' by the Beatles from the album *Sgt. Pepper's Lonely Hearts Club Band*. (William Kite performed in Fanque's Circus between 1843 and 1845.)

There were two platforms that were arranged in a V-shape with the ticket office on the north end, and there was a small garden situated between the two platforms. In 1851, a link was opened from the EUR line to the Norwich to Ely line. By 1854, the

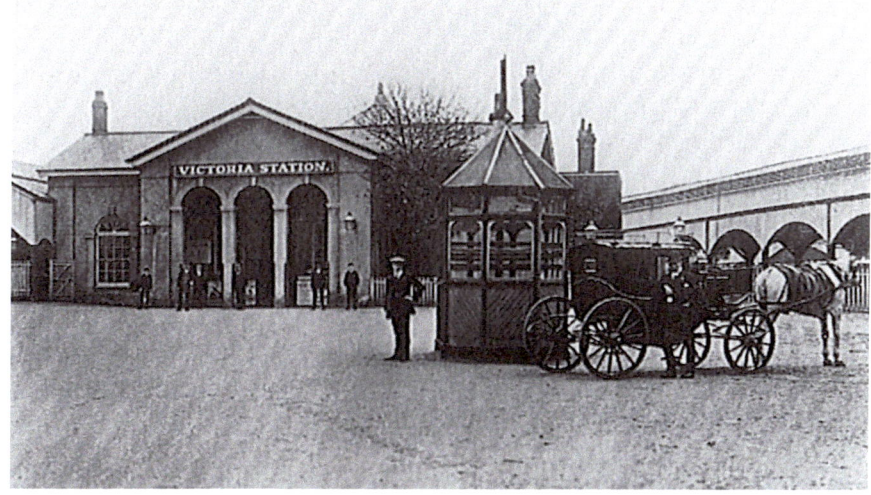

Victoria Station.

A–Z of Norwich

EUR was taken over by Eastern Counties Railways, but by the 1860s, railways in East Anglia were in financial difficulties, and the majority of them were then leased to the Eastern Counties Railways who had visions of amalgamating all of the stations but were refused the permission by the government. This changed in 1862 when the Great Eastern Railway came into force in which Thorpe (Norwich Station) and Victoria became GER stations.

The coal depot site is now a Sainsbury store and the trackbeds are now used by pedestrians.

R. Coller & Sons

The business started in King's Lynn in 1849, and in 1868, Richard Coller came to Norwich. In the 1870s, he became a member of the town council, and in 1876, he became mayor, and within eleven days he received King Edward VII and Queen Alexandra who were here to provide support for accommodation at the Norfolk and Norwich Hospital.

During his time as mayor, £2,000 was contributed to the distressed people of southern India. He became a Justice of the Peace in 1879 and remained a magistrate in the city even though he moved to Holland Park, Kensington, London. He was a director of many companies, including the Great Eastern Railway and the King's Lynn Docks and Railway.

George Arthur Coller joined the business in 1871 and was sheriff in 1895; he was also a director of Bullard & Sons Ltd. Charles Tarrant Coller joined in 1874 and was also a director of Crawshay & Youngs Ltd.

The head office was situated in St Stephens next to Victoria Station, and there were many branches all over the eastern counties. As well as running the wholesale and retail coal business, the company moved into developing corn and cake. They also had maltings in the eastern counties.

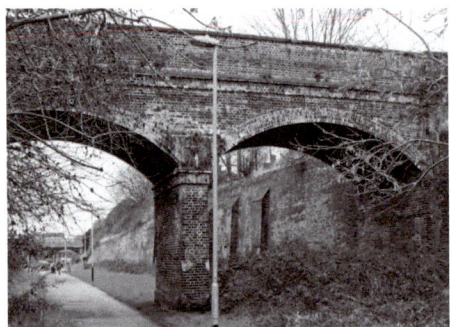 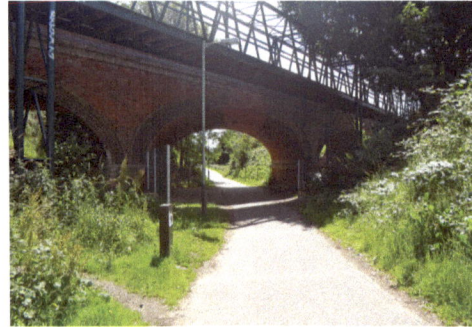

Above left: Victoria Station approach.

Above right: Hall Road Victoria Station underpass.

War Memorial

Norwich's war memorial, which also goes by the names Norwich Cenotaph or Norwich City War Memorial, was built as a memorial to the soldiers of the First World War. Unveiled in 1927, it was situated outside the Guildhall, and it moved to its present location in 1938 and was opened on 29 October 1938 by George VI. Designed by C. H. James and S. R. Piece, it originally had walls and gates. The architect Sir Edward Lutyens made Norwich the last of his eight cenotaphs in England. Before Sir Edward was involved, there were several designs for the memorial, and in 1926, Lord Mayor Charles Bignold wanted the design completed before he left office. He went on to establish the Joint Hospitals and War Memorial Appeal in memory of the dead to raise funds for the Norfolk and Norwich Hospital along with the Jenny Lind Children's Hospital.

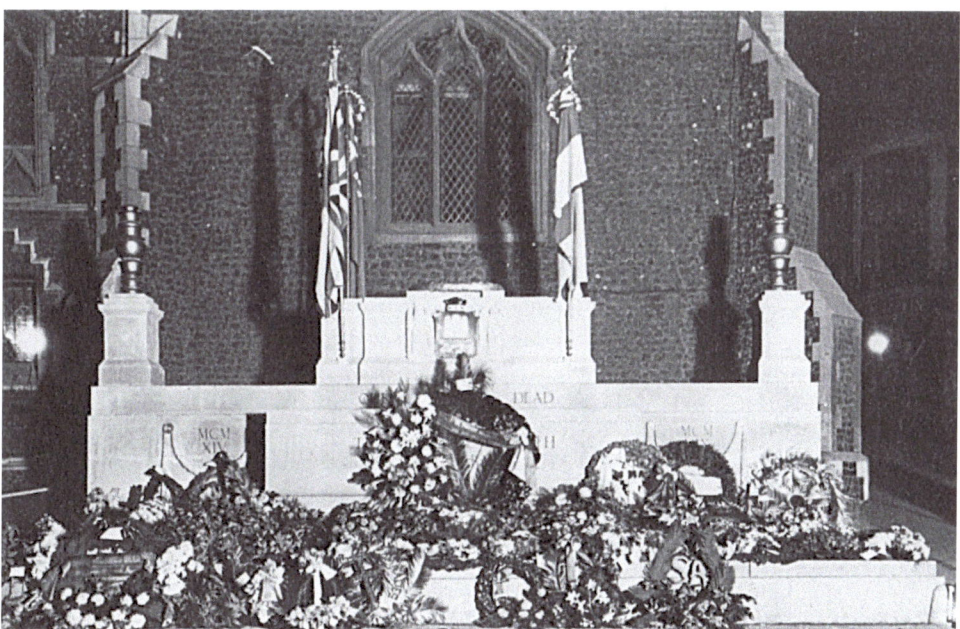

War Memorial, Guildhall.

Mayor Bignold wanted to raise £35,000 with £4,000 going towards the memorial. As there was no room to include all names, Sir Edward designed a roll of honour in which the names of Norwich's 3,544 dead are listed. It was placed in Norwich Castle in 1931.

The cost of the monument was £2,700 with a sum of £270 being paid to Sir Edward. Gen. Sir Ian Hamilton presided over the unveiling that was performed by Bertie Withers, a local veteran. Bertie joined up in September 1914 and fought in the Gallipoli Campaign and the first Battle of Gaza. Bertie suffered major injuries, losing a leg, and spent a year recuperating at the Norfolk and Norwich Hospital.

It closed in November 2004 when the undercroft was found to be unsound. Within a few years, ex-MP Martin Bell stated that you would have to visit war-torn Iraq to view a war memorial in such bad state. After years of the City Council trying to raise funds, a deal was struck in 2009 when the Homes and Communities Agency agreed to the funding. To make sure that the gardens and memorial were placed in exactly the same position, English Heritage was called in to assist.

Norwich City Council worked together on the project with NPS Property Consultants, R. G. Carter, The Landscape Partnership, Stirling Maynard and Fairhaven and Woods.

On Wednesday 16 March 2011, the reopening of the Norwich Memorial Gardens took place. Many people gathered for this historic opening with eighty-four-year-old Victor Howe, president of the Norwich branch of the Royal British Legion and twenty-year-old David Heir, serving with the 1st Battalion of the Royal Anglian Regiment, cutting the ribbon. The gardens had been closed for six years.

The memorial has been crafted from Portland stone, and the sarcophagus has gilded flambeaux at each end with the city coat of arms placed in the middle.

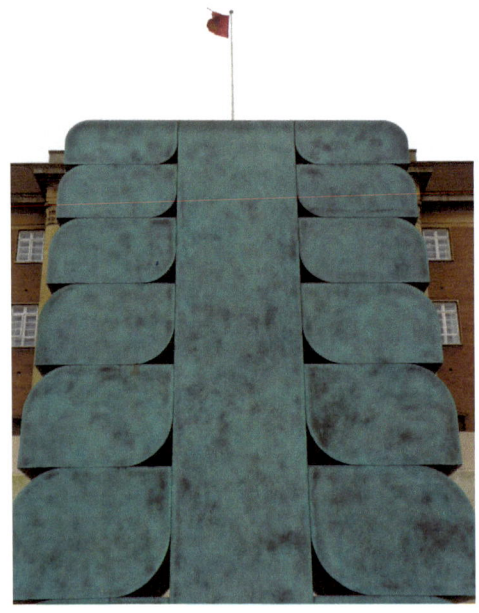

'Breath'.

Also new is a bronze sculpture by Paul de Monchaux called 'Breath', which was chosen from a shortlist by the Memorial Gardens' Steering Group. The sculpture reads, 'The living honour the dead, only a breath divides them.'

Norwich City Cllr Steve Morphew said at the time of the opening that refurbishment and reopening of the new war memorial had been a long time coming, and it was fantastic to see the project bearing fruit.

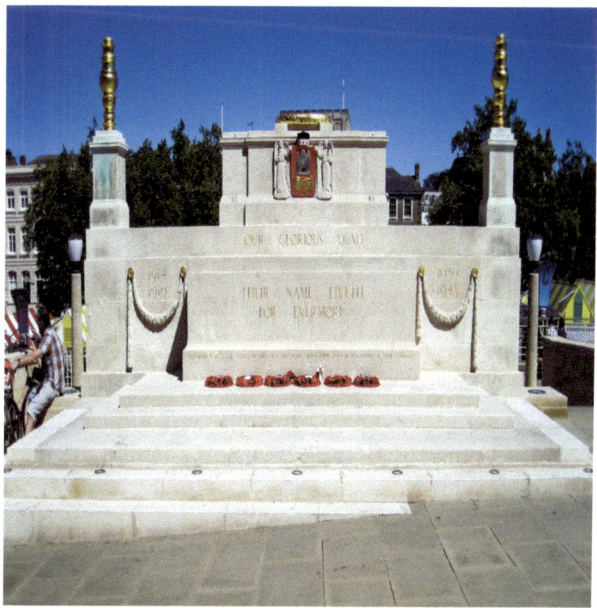

War Memorial.

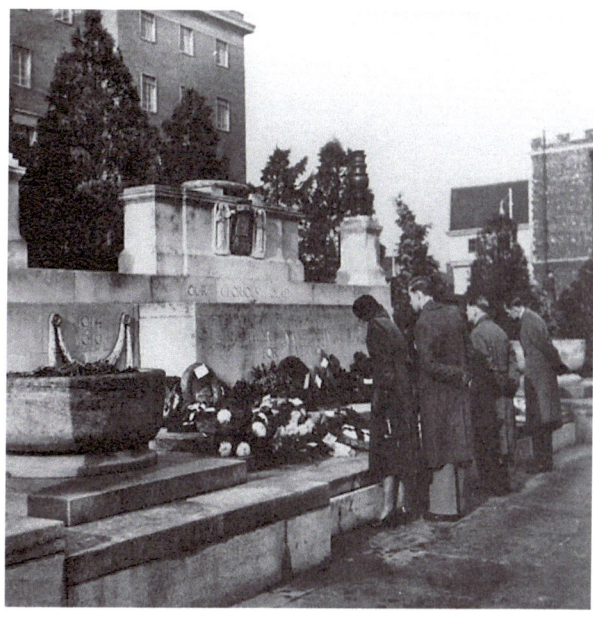

War Memorial wreaths, Norwich.

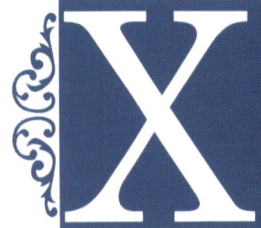

The X Bells

The Ten Bells dates back to the 1700s, and it is said that if you stand on the roof, you will be able to see ten public houses. Its first two landlords, John Brett (1760–62) and Richard Knights (1763–64), were worsted weavers. The house has recently been rebranded as X Bells. It now has a gin distillery and bottling room, which is a joint investment with Greene King Brewery. The distillery will produce two 43 per cent ABV London dry gins. The company that is owned by Redwell Brewery has revived Bullard beers. The gins have the names Bullards Norwich gin and Firewater gin. At one stage, Bullards had over 500 public houses in Norwich, and the name is built into the foundations of Norwich history.

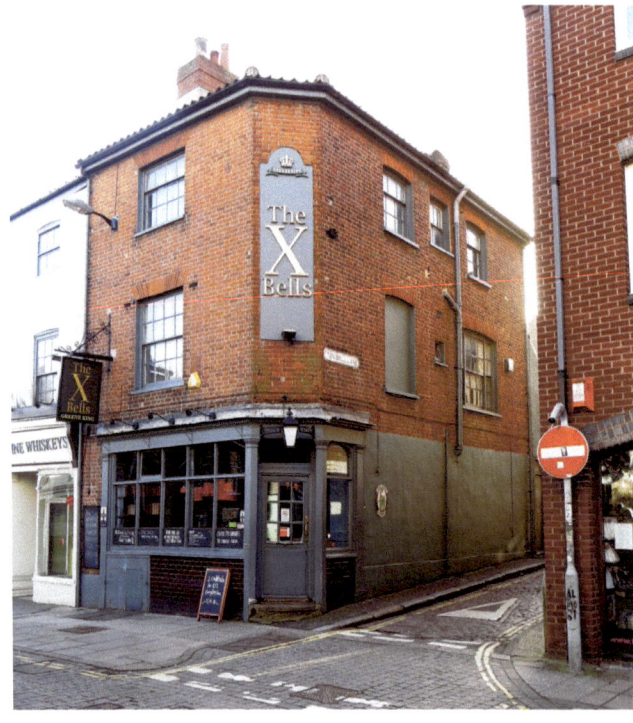

Ten Bells Pub.

X

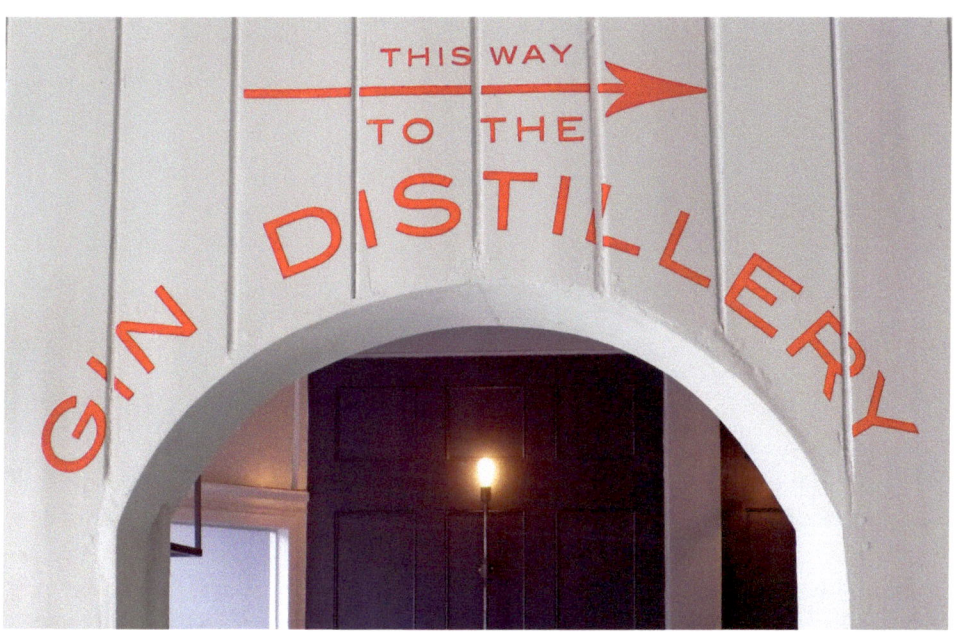

Above: Ten Bells' Pub gin distillery sign.
Right: Ten Bells' Pub gin distillery.
Below: Ten Bells' pavement plaque.

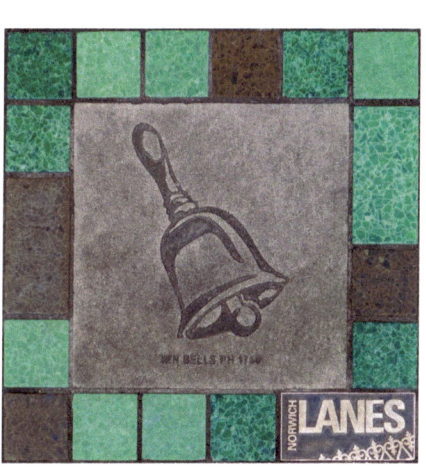

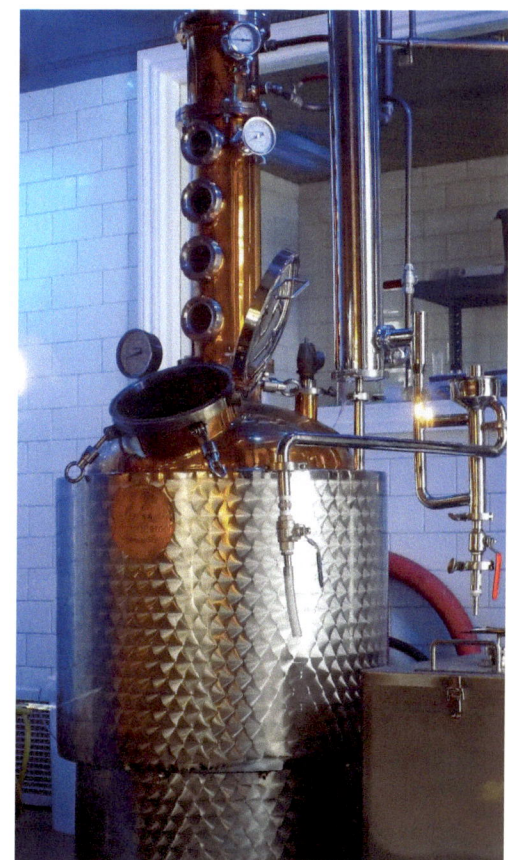

Y

Yards and Courts

When the city walls were built, there was a lot of open land; some was kept that way, but most was turned into an array of gardens, stables, courtyards and private areas. These lands were entered through openings in the streets. By the seventeenth and eighteenth centuries, the yards and courts became overpopulated, and this caused severe overcrowding and sanitary problems. As Norwich expanded itself outside of the city walls, terraced houses were built to solve part of the problem. It was said that by 1900, Norwich had about 750 yards, but in the 1920s, housing estates started to be built, Mile Cross being the first. Today, a majority of the yards and courts have been transformed into luxury housing, something that could not have been dreamed of centuries ago.

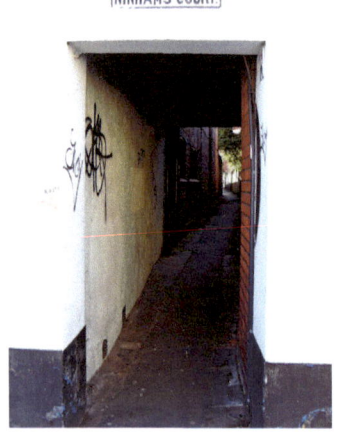 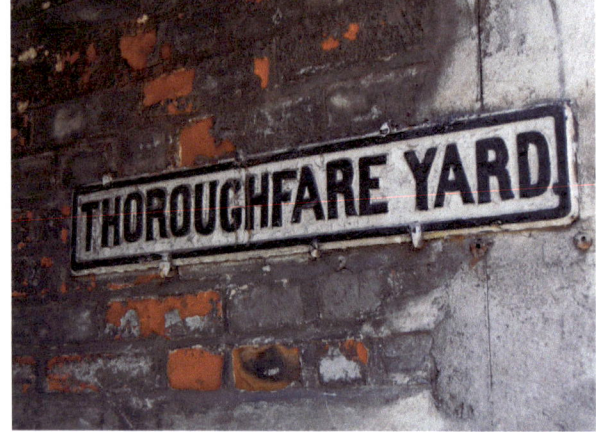

Above left: Ninhams Court.

Above right: Thoroughfare Yard.

Z

Zeppelin

In 1915, the Kaiser gave the orders for the bombing of military targets along the British coast, but not London, by Zeppelin airships.

The Zeppelin *L4*, which was under the command of Kapitanleutnant Count Magnus von Platen-Hallermund, had dropped bombs over Sheringham and Hunstanton along the north Norfolk cost. The Kapitanleutnant ended up in Norwich, but by that time, he had run out of bombs. Norwich was one of the first cities to have blackouts ordered. In all, there were sixty Zeppelin air raids, but no bombs fell on the city.

Appendix

There are many interesting old Norwich legal customs that just could not be placed within the A–Z title, so I have placed them in an appendix and very much hope that you will enjoy and learn from them.

In the cases of homicide, housebreaking or a felony that takes place within the city, if the criminal is found within the boundaries, the person has to be kept in prison without bail until the case is brought to court.

If a person is committed for murder in the city, suburbs or river, then 'englishry' cannot be claimed as the king's charter is exempted the city from 'murdrum'.

All accusations of felony have to be made in the county court.

If thieves who find themselves arrested from a complaint by a party in the city are in possession of known stolen goods, they can be judged in the city court before coroners and bailiffs. This also applies even if the theft was committed outside the city as long as the complainant comes forward. If there is no complaint, the city must not try the thieves but has the legal right to hold them in prison until the justices of gaol have the cases tried in the city court.

Whether it be day or night, when hue-and-cry is raised in the city for any felony, the complaint regarding the crime must be lodged straight away by men who are subjects of the king until the person pursued is captured or offers an attachment for answering the charges that the person is accused of in court.

For felons who come to a city church and decide to remain there until they abjure the realm, any goods they have at the time of the abjuration are to be appraised to the use of the king and then delivered by the coroner to the citizen who will then become answerable to them to the itinerant justices. If the felon has property in the city, then its value for a year will be appraised for the use of the king.

If a criminal or one who has abjured the realm makes their way back to the city without the king's permission and fails to surrender themselves, they will be pursued with hue-and-cry and can be made a subject to immediate judgement without having the need to detain them.

People who enter the city who are classed as outsiders who act in a suspicious manner are to be immediately arrested by either the bailiffs or constables and then held until security is given and a promise to uphold the king's peace.

When a person in the city is drowned, whether it be in the waterways, wells or pits or in the river going as far as Breydon Water, then the coroner is to view the location and to hold an inquest. If no foul play is shown, then the body will be released for immediate burial.

Appendix

If a fight takes place and one person is injured, the person causing the injury is to be held in prison until the attacked person's wounds heal, also, the attacker has to forfeit the weapon used to the bailiff and to offer compensation to the wounded as well as being amerced (fined) and punished for the crime of breaking the peace. If blood has been spilt, then the attacker is placed under arrest until the attacked person sues him and for the attacker to give guarantees.

Disputes over ownership of borough tenement are proceeded with three summons and three distraints that are made during fortnightly intervals on the tenant. If at any time the tenant defaults in answering the questions, the tenement can be taken into the king's hands.

When a plea by a writ of entry or of trespass is filed in the king's courts, jurisdiction over it is always claimed for the city courts. Pleas held in the king's court in London result in citizens having to pay expenses having been told to serve on inquests and juries (which is why there was the need for cases to be dealt within the city).

In pleas that are initiated by the king's writ where sessions are permitted, and the party is able to provide reason why he is unable to appear, he is given a seven-day stay, failure of which will result in the person being greatly amerced and still forced to answer all charges put to him.

With pleas resulting to the construction of a wall, house, drain or a ditch that causes a nuisance to neighbour's properties are to be served with a king's writ, followed by a summons.

Where city custom treats like novel disseisin by a fresh force then the land in question is to be seized by the king's own hand with the tenant being removed. (The Assize of 'novel disseisin' was a fast way of getting seized land back.)

Legal concerns regarding tenements in the city are governed by city customs and city courts and because tenements can be freely bequeathed, probate from the last testament of the persons bequeathing these tenements is made at the city courts before the bailiffs, and this would be followed by a probate in ecclesiastical court.

If a spinster acquired property in the city before getting married, she is able to bequeath the property to whomever she so wishes, which does not have to be her husband, unless she had her husband's child after the marriage.

Where a property jointly owned by man and wife is bequeathed by the husband to the wife for her lifetime and afterwards to go to some other legatee and his heirs, if the wife has ratified the testament after the death of her husband, or was its executrix, or has shown to have consented to her husband's bequest, then the wife can have no future claim on the bequeathed property.

In a plea of debt, regardless of the amount between peers of the city, the debtor would be summoned to appear a day after the plaintiff made the complaint. If the debtor is known to be a freeman, he is given eight days to answer, and if he fails, then he is to be distrained, but if he appears after that he is still given the eight days. Failure after that he is to incur a penalty until he attaches himself.

In a plea between a peer of the city and a foreigner, whether with or without the king's writ, at the time of judgement, the proof of the peer is to hold good over the word of the foreigner.

If the employ of a bailiff is not to hand, then it becomes lawful for the services of a comburgess (freeman) to attach the goods of a debtor who is trying to avoid him. The comburgess must not retain any person but must bring it to the attention of the bailiffs straight away and to be attached to prosecute the debtor.

To undertake the assize of bread, there needed to be four honest and law-abiding men, with two of them bakers and two knowledgeable in what was required by the city and country and are elected each year. In front of the city community, they take an oath to keep the assize. They are to buy corn, have it ground, shifted and baked into bread, which they shall then sell to the populace. No baker in the city is allowed to sell bread until the bread of the assize had been sold. (This was done twice a year after Michaelmas and after Easter.) If at any time divergent measure is found, it is permanently confiscated by the bailiffs and punished as the offence warrants.

Ells and weights that were used by the merchants of the city for buying and selling are, between two to four times a year, to be examined by the bailiffs to see if they are accurate and reliable, and if so they are stamped with a seal. Those found to be inaccurate are confiscated and destroyed, as with all unreliable measures discovered in the city.

No resident of the city may engage in commerce, unless he is at scot and lot and contributes to the aids imposed on the community ('scot and lot' describes a taxpaying householder). Those accepted as a peer of the city are to be of free status. Those who are admitted are to undergo the entrance ceremony before at least twelve of those assigned by the community each year to this task, at one of the four set dates each year; if a lesser number is present, applicants may not be admitted. If the applicant is a foreigner and has not been apprenticed in the city, he must pay at least 20s.

No comburgess or any other resident of the city or its suburbs, nor anyone at all, may on any day in the year buy for purposes of resale to others any foodstuffs in the market, on the quay, on the river, in a house, courtyard, street, lane or at any location in the city, nor make a bargain to buy such items by giving God's penny, until the bell has been rung for the mass of the Blessed Virgin in the Church of Holy Trinity. No one may, in any road, street, lane or other place in the city or suburb, nor within one league outside by land or water, intercept such foods being brought to the city, for sale, with the purpose of buying them before they reach the public marketplace so that the goods are sold for a higher price than they ought to be; no one who brings victuals to the city may in any way be impeded from being able to sell them freely in the market to anyone wishing to buy. If the bailiffs find anyone in contravention of this, or if any reputable man makes a complaint about such an offence, and the accused is convicted, then he must be heavily amerced by the bailiffs and any compliant is to be awarded damages, but if the offender is then convicted of the same offence a second time, then all his products are to be confiscated and the city court to sentence him

Appendix

to the pillory. If the same offender is again convicted, he shall be punished as before and also abjure the city for one year and one day along with paying damages to the complainant.

Trading in the city is a common right of all peers of the city, but certain persons contrary to city custom have the practice of using several of their servants, or others whom they claim to be their servants or representatives, in order to purchase multiple shares in products to the disadvantage of peers. Therefore, no one is to make purchases except personally or through a single servant only; his fellow citizens who may wish to join in purchasing the same products are not prevented from having an equal share, as they ought.

No peers of the city may take his servant as a partner for purpose of buying and selling, unless the servant makes entry as a peer, nor may the servant be represented as an apprentice in order to make profit for his master. Anyone convicted of this shall pay a fine of 40s to be delivered to the Chamberlain for the use of the city.

Where there has been the need to hold a common assembly for the benefit of the city, some comburgesses have not bothered to obey the summons to come and deal with community business, with the result that much business cannot be dealt with, to the detriment of the city.

To ensure that every craft or industry in the city is carried out properly and honestly without any fraud that might cause scandal to the city, each year the bailiffs and the twenty-four elected by the community shall choose between two and four of the more prominent and trustworthy of each industry or craft. They are sworn to the Gospels to conduct an honest and comprehensive search of the industry or craft, without sparing anyone, at least four times a year – more if need arises – so that no fraud, deceit or falsehood can be maintained by the practitioners. If they discover any such offence, they are to inform the bailiffs and the twenty-four elected in the name of the community, who are to amend the problem, except compensation, and punish the guilty in order to set an example to others and to restore the city's good name.

Sergeants who plead on behalf of clients in the court of which they are officers are to uphold the laws and customs of the city and shall not for any client, outsider or other, make arguments contrary to those customs. They are to take oath before the bailiffs each Michaelmas. They shall not, in court, speak of their associates nor their adversary in a defamatory or dishonourable way, nor stir up bad feelings, but rather serve their clients in a good and honest manner. If any acts contrary to this and continues in such behaviour after three warnings to desist and behave honourably, he shall be suspended from pleading the case until he amends his behaviour and wins back into the good graces of the community.

Those peers whom the community elects as bailiffs of the city may not refuse to take up the burden of office, under the ancient penalty of 40s paid to the community. Which fine the bailiffs then in office are to quickly levy from everyone who refuse, unless they change their mind within three days and accept the office. Once a fine is levied, the appointed electors shall choose another suitable person in the place of him.

Each year on the day of their election, the bailiffs are to swear an oath on the Gospels to observe and maintain all this.

Upon their election each year, the city bailiffs will take oath that:

1. They will serve the king faithfully in that office of having custody of the city.
2. They will treat the people of the city properly, giving equal justice to rich and poor.
3. They will uphold and maintain the laws, liberties and customs of the city in all matters.
4. They will faithfully acquit the city of its obligation by paying in full its fee farm.
5. They will execute judgement of the city court in all points, as specified by city custom, sparing no one.
6. They will not permit any foreigner to stay in the city conducting commerce as through a peer of the city, unless he first makes solemn entry before those elected by the community to administer that.
7. If they are informed of anyone conducting commerce in the city contrary to the above, they will have his goods seized and put in safekeeping until he pays a penalty for the offence and swears not to commit the act again without becoming a peer of the city to which he is to be compelled, if he wishes to remain in the city.